AN INTRODUCTION TO
WRITINGMUSIC
FORTELEVISION

The Art & Technique of TV Music Writing
With Contributions From Emmy® Award Winning Composers

MICHAEL**KRUK**

FUNDAMENTAL**CHANGES**

An Introduction to Writing Music For TV

The Art & Technique of TV Music Writing
With Contributions From Emmy® Award Winning Composers

ISBN: 978-1-78933-055-7

Published by **www.fundamental-changes.com**

Copyright © 2019 Michael Kruk

Edited by Tim Pettingale

www.fundamental-changes.com

Twitter: @guitar_joseph

Over 10,000 fans on Facebook: **FundamentalChangesInGuitar**

Instagram: **FundamentalChanges**

If you're inspired to explore composing for TV further, visit

www.musicforincome.com/introbook

Dedicated to my mum, Elizabeth Kruk, for your continuing love and support over the years.

Cover Image Copyright: Shutterstock: PrinceOfLove

Contents

Introduction

Over the last two decades, TV shows have upped their ante. Whether it's a stunning nature documentary, or a riveting, multi-million-dollar drama, productions for the small screen captivate global audiences and continue to become more and more impressive.

These shows can vary widely in the genres of music used for their soundtracks, but for their scores, certain compositional tools, tricks and techniques hold true. TV composers are often required to create sonic worlds for TV shows that would be effective in films intended for cinema audiences.

In this book, you'll learn the real-world techniques needed to effectively compose and produce music for TV. You'll notice that many of the topics covered are expansive subjects; they could be (and some are) the subject of books in their own right. My aim is to not bog you down with too much theory, or trudge through every facet of each topic, but to give you the essential tools you need. Many successful TV composers are not masters of every discipline – but they *have* mastered the skills they need and picked up useful tips along the way.

At the heart of this book are usable, practical ideas and techniques that you can apply directly to creating soundtracks that work for TV shows, avoiding the mistakes that so many TV composers make when starting out.

You'll discover that not being intrusive is key, as music is often not the main focus in a TV show.

You'll learn how composers' soundtracks can be incredibly effective tools to tell a story and set the tone for a program.

You'll read about some of the most usable and effective approaches to begin composing and producing music for TV.

Included are some great starting points for generating ideas, whilst ensuring your music stays true to the tried and tested composition concepts for TV soundtracks – rules you can experiment with breaking later, if you choose, as long as everything you do serves the story.

Definitions

Finally, a note about terminology:

While an editor has a fixed role as the person who cuts and syncs the music to the pictures, the roles of director, producer and show runner can sometimes overlap and the boundaries are frequently blurred. This is confusing for first time composers and personally I've had to answer to people in all of these roles. Throughout this book, when I refer to these job titles or "the production team", I am simply citing the main decision maker to whom I'm reporting on a project.

Any reference to "he" or "she" pertaining to people in these roles should be read as interchangeable, unless a specific person is being referred to.

In this book, a "cue" is interchangeable with a "track" or a "piece" of music. All these terms refer to a piece of music you are writing for a TV show.

Contributors

My background is as a documentary composer and I have scored shows that have been aired all over the world – from cute animal documentaries, to award-winning productions narrated by David Attenborough, to multi-part series for the BBC Natural History Unit.

The entire process of making a documentary – as well as creating its score – can differ slightly from the processes of other TV genres. In fact, the approach may differ from documentary to documentary! With this in mind, it was really important to me that you received the best information from expert composers who work in different fields. As a result, you can read insider tips on composing across a wide range of genres, as well as learning a variety of approaches. To that end, I'm delighted that three world class contributors have been generous in sharing insights from their wealth of expertise and were willing to impart great practical advice to augment this book.

Michael Price (*Sherlock, The Unforgotten*) and Mac Quayle (*Mr. Robot, Feud*) share their experiences and findings from scoring major TV dramas. Walter Murphy (*Family Guy, American Dad*), shares tips from having scored two of the best-loved animations on television. Between them they have a slew of major award wins and nominations, including four Emmys® and Academy Awards.

You'll find full biographies for each contributor at the back of the book.

Have fun!

Michael Kruk

Get the Audio

The audio files for this book are available to download for free from **www.fundamental-changes.com.** The link is in the top right-hand corner. Simply select this book title from the drop-down menu and follow the instructions to get the audio.

We recommend that you download the files directly to your computer, not to your tablet, and extract them there before adding them to your media library. You can then put them on your tablet, iPod or burn them to CD. On the download page there is a help PDF and we also provide technical support via the contact form.

For over 350 Free Guitar Lessons with Videos Check out:

www.fundamental-changes.com

Twitter: **@guitar_joseph**

Over 10,000 fans on Facebook: **FundamentalChangesInGuitar**

Instagram: **FundamentalChanges**

If You're Inspired to Explore Composing for TV Further, Visit

www.musicforincome.com/introbook

All Music Copyright © 2019 Michael Kruk

Chapter One – Creating a Palette

Before composing a single note, it's important to understand your role in the greater scheme of a project. What actually is the job of a TV composer? First and foremost, you are part of a storytelling team – you just happen to be working with music. The whole production team is in the business of telling a compelling story. Your colleagues are doing that via images, sound effects and narration. Once the team has understood the arc of the story and the moods at play, the tasks of writing and recording the music can begin. Never forget this important first step and don't rush to get into the composition stage. This is so important to understand, I want to repeat it:

First and foremost, you are part of the storytelling team – you just happen to be working with music.

The first challenge a TV composer is faced with is to create a sonic world that enhances the storytelling. You need to consider how you will build a palette of sounds that supports the *feel* of the show and illuminates the story being told.

Your decisions in this area may be (but are not always), influenced by the era of the show, its geographical location(s), or any number of factors the production team deems relevant. Choices made at this stage will contribute hugely to establishing the tone of the whole production. For this reason, it's best to do most experimentation *before* the project advances and you're in the thick of writing cues. Michael Price says,

> *"If you're on a ten-days-per-episode, quick, TV type schedule, then you haven't got time to start exploring when you're in the middle of it… it tends to be however long you can bolt on at the front of it.*
>
> *And I do find if I haven't done any exploring, even if it's just for a day, and if I've just opened up an old template from a show… you just find yourself naturally repeating yourself, which isn't a great feeling.*
>
> *So, I do work hard to find some of that time, even if it's a bit compressed."*

Conditioning

Other elements will come into play when creating a palette, but a good place to begin is to narrow down a selection of instruments that will work together to create the right mood. Mac Quayle says,

> *"It all starts with a conversation with the producers or creators of the series or film. We talk about what the sound might be and from there some ideas about instrumentation may come out of those conversations.*
>
> *Sometimes they say they'd like to try a particular instrument, or they'll say that one of the instruments I've chosen isn't working for them and could I try something else."*

Before we discuss how to create an effective world for your project, think about what different instruments can mean in the context of soundtrack music. Over the years, we've been conditioned to interpret sounds in a particular way. Certain sounds and instruments have come to represent different moods. For example, if I play fast 1/16th notes on a Hi-Hat over a scene, the chances are you'll feel a sense of urgency and tension. A slow, solo bugle will often conjure a sombre, reflective mood, perhaps with regal or military connotations.

We are so used to hearing certain instruments used in this way that it's hard to pull them away from these moods. They just make most audiences feel and react in a specific way. Don't see this as a restriction. In fact, it's brilliant! Many instruments are instant mood generators you can incorporate into your palette, knowing they will generally make people feel a certain way.

That said, such instrument/mood associations can be the reason your music *doesn't work* for some directors or producers. They may have conditioning of their own at play.

I heard a story about a composer who had written a beautiful track for a scene featuring the main tune on clarinet. The director couldn't tell the composer exactly why it didn't work for him. He liked the piece of music, but something was "off". A whole load of rewriting ensued, as the composer tried to unravel the cause of the issue, but to no avail; the track was replaced.

Fast forward to the wrap party and in a conversation over a bottle of wine, the director spoke about his upbringing. He told a group of people at the party (which included the composer), how he was forced to play the clarinet at school and had always hated it. Imagine the composer's reaction! All he'd needed to do was not use a clarinet! Of course, it was impossible to figure that out when even the director didn't realise his own conditioning was coloring his preferences.

Sometimes the choice of instrument can make or break a cue. It can be the sole reason that a track works or doesn't work. After considering the mood of the story, the choice of instrumentation is the next biggest factor. This is the advantage of creating an instrumental palette ahead of time. Doing this preparation beforehand decreases the chance of you being rejected by producers/directors based on your instrument choices. Walter Murphy offers the following insight:

> *"When Family Guy started in 1999, we experimented with tone a little. For instance, the way Family Guy is set up is that some character says some outrageous thing and then you cut to the exterior of the house, as if nothing happened. So, we decided we were going to play music as if nothing happened; we were going to completely ignore what Peter Griffin [Family Guy character] just said.*
>
> *I did little jazzy versions of snippets of the theme song, and after about the second episode, I did one with the Flugelhorns and Flutes an octave higher, and Seth said, 'I love that! That's great!' So that became the sound of that part of the show each week. And now that we've made that a thing, it's kind of a signature."*

Established Palettes: Pros and Cons

Specific TV genres often have an established palette of instruments associated with their soundtracks. This is both a blessing and a curse to a composer contracted to score a TV show.

It's a blessing in the sense that it's nice to have a fall-back – something you know will "just work" for that genre. I can pretty much guarantee that at some point in your career, when you need to deliver a cue at the last minute, you will be quietly grateful for a "just add water" solution! If you're asked to make a cue more tense, more comedic, darker etc., you can reach for one of these elements to add the right seasoning to your track and it will most likely take it in the right direction.

What is challenging is that some genres are so wed to a particular sonic palette that it's tricky to break free from it and create something original. If you want to break away from the norm (remembering to explore this in the early stages of the project), I encourage you to let the project be your guide. How does the production you're working on differ to other mainstream shows in this genre? What elements of the story – its era, location, point of view, the way the film is shot, or some other aspect – will allow you to sympathetically move slightly out of the expected palette?

Don't try this for the sake of it. Remember our mantra:

First and foremost, you are part of the storytelling team – you just happen to be working with music.

Make sure you have an angle and something to say.

Example Mood Palettes

What follows is a list of several common TV moods and genres, together with some frequently used instrument palettes for each. There will be times when this is all a program needs for its palette, but when you are in the early stages of creating your own palette for a program, you can use this a starting point from which to explore.

It's worth pointing out that the outlines below are generalisations – they are certainly not the only palette choices that can achieve these moods. Note too, that for TV underscore,[1] the melody component is often not necessary.

Action / Pursuit / Chase

- Melody: Electric guitar; brass section.

- Accompaniment: Electric guitar chugs; staccato strings; brass stabs; pulsing synths.

- Rhythmic elements: 1/16th note Hi-Hats or shakers; driving drums or electronic loops.

Example 1a:

---

1. "Underscore" refers to music played quietly under dialogue or a visual scene.

Ominous / Scary

- Melody: Bowed glass; bowed piano string; often more textural than melodic.

- Accompaniment: Low strings; tremolo strings; low drones; "hollow" synth pads with clashing notes/harmonies.

- Rhythmic elements: Usually none as these cues are quite ambient; the odd percussion/drum hit drenched in reverb may add atmosphere!

Example 1b:

Tension

- Melody: Sparse piano; electric guitar; often more textural than melodic.

- Accompaniment: Held high tremolo string notes; held synth pad notes; ominous 1/8th note low strings; pulsing or rhythmic synths; swells; low drones.

- Rhythmic elements: Sparse electronic loops; elements mimicking ticking clocks or time passing.

Example 1c:

Panoramic / Nature / Awe

- Melody: Violin section; brass.

- Accompaniment: String ostinatos; high staccato woodwinds.

- Rhythmic elements: Large drums (e.g. Taiko drums) playing simple but driving rhythms.

Example 1d:

Magic / Wonder / Fantasy

- Melody: Glockenspiel; celeste; female choir; flute.

- Accompaniment: Strings – *arco* (played with the bow) or *pizzicato*; choir; harp.

- Rhythmic elements: Triangle; light cymbals.

Example 1e:

Emotional Drama / Tearjerker / Tender / Tragedy

- Melody: Sparse piano; cello or other solo string instrument; solo voice.

- Accompaniment: Simple synth pad; strings; piano

- Rhythmic elements: Often none or simple soft pulsing synth pad.

Example 1f:

Feelgood / Light-hearted

- Melody: Piano; light bells.

- Accompaniment: Acoustic guitar(s); mandolin; ukulele; pizzicato strings.

- Rhythmic elements: Shakers; light percussion; hand claps; light drum kit.

Example 1g:

Dramedy (A combination of drama and comedy, often quite mischievous!)

- Melody: Pizzicato strings; clarinet; bassoon.

- Accompaniment: Pizzicato strings; marimba; vibraphone; light use of piano.

- Rhythmic elements: Shakers; triangle; bongos.

Example 1h:

Kids TV

- Melody: Xylophone, marimba, glockenspiel or other tuned percussion; light bells; flutes; piano; whistling.

- Accompaniment: Marimba; pizzicato strings; piano; tuba (for basslines).

- Rhythmic elements: Woodblocks; hand claps; classroom percussion.

Example 1i:

A Note About Comedy

You'll notice that I've not included "comedy" in the above genres/moods. This is because it's rare (outside of kids cartoons), that TV comedy shows are scored with obviously comedic music. Comedy is often much more effective when the music is scored "straight." Check this out the next time you see a comedy scene on TV with accompanying music. Hence, the closest we get to this is "Dramedy".

The Constant Quest For "New" and "Fresh"

Amongst other descriptions, you can bet your bottom dollar that TV directors and producers will frequently use the words "new" and "fresh" when describing what they want from a soundtrack. There are several ways to deliver this.

One way is to provide an interesting and fresh combination of instruments. Another way is to find an angle to the story such that an unlikely choice of sound palette works for the soundtrack.

Let me give you an example. Maybe you find that a soft Reggae feel perfectly juxtaposes the story of a stressed-out businessman working in his city office, precisely because his dream is to retire to a sun-drenched island. I'm not suggesting you try this exact approach, but for the sake of argument, let's say that it works. Breaking the "genre rules" in a way that truly serves the story, without drawing too much attention to the music, can lead to a unique score. I've seen such "fresh" approaches lead to award nominations.

You'll often need to have footage before you can try out such an approach and, whatever you do (especially at the start of your career), talk through any such brainwaves with the person you're reporting to. Don't wait until the music delivery deadline before springing your curveball Reggae idea! But, don't rule out a left-field idea either. Just make 100% sure that it serves the story or offers a relevant point of view. Always discuss it with the creative time ahead of time.

Another method many TV composers utilise successfully to keep a score fresh is the manipulation of sounds and instruments. By "instruments" I also mean all the weird and wonderful sounds and samples that can be produced (or imported) in your Digital Audio Workstation (DAW).

Manipulating Sounds

"If you've got time, then it's lovely to spend two or three days going through a bunch of your sample libraries and reminding yourself of what you've got. Often, we end up with far too many sounds that we can't remember. I've got no idea [what I've got]! You might think 'I've got no memory of buying this', but it might work for this project." – Michael Price

I'm sure it's no surprise to you that most music for TV these days is generated electronically. Many composers favor such a production-led approach. The manipulation of synths and samples, as well as acoustic instruments, can lead to the fresh edge your producer/director is looking for.

Some of the tools that TV composers have found most effective to create distinctive, fresh sounds at the time of writing are:

- Reversing sounds and instrumental performances (i.e. playing audio waveforms or samples backwards). Most DAWs give you a one-click option to do this to audio. We'll talk about reversing sounds in more detail later in this book.

- Distortion and saturation. This is commonplace on electric guitar, but can be used effectively elsewhere to create an unsettling texture. A little often goes a long way.

- Granular synthesis. This is essentially the process of fragmenting audio into many small 'grains' – each grain can then receive its own processing and even be re-ordered. Some music software allows you to import your own audio, then manipulate it at a granular level. You can make interesting and subtle changes or twist and warp a sound source to within an inch of its life!

- Guitar pedals. Running instruments other than guitars through guitar pedal chains can result it some interesting and unique textures.

Looping, compression and reverb are also popular tools – used independently or in conjunction with the above techniques.

Other than simply providing a new dimension to a soundtrack, when it's done well, a distinctive manipulated sound can take on a life of its own, sometimes serving a distinct purpose. Imagine, for instance, a high, unsettling violin harmonic, slightly distorted and pulsing. This could become an effective *leitmotif*[2] in itself when connected to a certain character or mood.

Remember though, while experimenting in this way is fun, always keep the end goal in mind!

Create a Template

Once you've settled on a combination of sounds, perhaps sketched out your first musical ideas, and feel that the production team are happy with the sound palette, it's time to create a template for the show in your DAW. This simply means saving these instruments, samples and settings in your DAW so you can instantly recall the palette when writing new cues.

To do this, use the "Save As" command in your DAW and name your new project file something like "Somber Detective Palette" (should you find yourself scoring a drama centered around a somber detective!)

Composers can differ in how they work with their palettes/templates, so let's consider some different approaches to organizing your work.

When writing a new cue, you might always begin by loading up your "Somber Detective Palette" template, even if you're not sure this new cue will use all of the same instruments. This approach can be effective if you find you can utilize one or two instruments from your palette for different cues and has two added benefits: first, it saves time when writing new material; second, it helps to create a unified sound across the show.

Multiple Palettes

If, however, you know a cue is going to be considerably different from others, you may need to consider multiple palettes and therefore multiple templates, as Walter Murphy points out:

"Since the two series I've mainly been doing since 1999 – Family Guy and American Dad – are basically orchestral scores with a live orchestra recording every week, I have a big orchestral palette to demo from at home.

"But then I also have several other palettes. I have a Rock/Pop palette and an EDM [Electronic Dance Music] set up as there's usually source music[3] in the shows – for example, when somebody goes into a disco or nightclub.

"Also, Family Guy is always making fun of, or parodying, some other pop-cultural show or movie. So, when they're making fun of Star Trek, I'm asked to write something that could have been the score to Star Trek in the '60s, or one of the Star Trek movies or something like that."

---

2. A leitmotif is a short recurring musical phrase, associated with a particular person, place or idea.

3. "Source Music" is any music that the characters in the show can hear themselves. Underscore isn't source music as the characters cannot hear it in real life.

It's possible that a show's soundtrack will have some vastly different musical feels, even within itself. Some of the nature documentaries I've scored have demanded the transition from a lioness hunting her prey, to returning to mother her cubs. Then the action will move on to the story of a totally different animal in that part of the world.

To tackle a project like this, I might set up a couple of palettes and have templates for each. It wouldn't be appropriate to rely on one palette, as you might if you were scoring a drama, set in one location, with a small, intimate cast.

Palette Case Study: Mexico Documentary

When I was working on a BBC Natural History series about Mexico, I had one template that I made from the instruments used for the title track. This was a large-scale orchestral piece with bold Mexican flavours added. Any similar bold orchestral track started with this template.

I also had two instruments that were important in terms of writing several other cues. The first was a Spanish guitar sample set to which I'd added EQ to warm it up, a fair bit of reverb and some delay. This came out for most of the intimate sounding cues.

The other was a simple, hollow sounding synth pad with just a little sparkle behind it. It was used throughout the series for scenes in underground caves and underwater sequences. If anything magical or "other worldly" was needed, out came this pad.

I set up another template with both these instruments in, ready for the more atmospheric cues.

This spawned a more generic template. If I'd featured an instrument in a few cues, then I would add it to my "General Mexico" template. I often then began new cues using that template. I also loved the fact that if I was halfway through a track and wondering which instrument to choose next, I could glance down the list in my DAW and immediately be reminded of the most obvious, and perhaps relevant, options.

For this project, I created my palettes around mood/genre as well as having a generic template. As I mentioned earlier, characters, locations and a multitude of other factors will dictate how your palettes differ, but I enjoyed using the constantly evolving "General Mexico" palette to write the cues. Some of the most magical moments came when I was able to effectively blend sounds from one or two cues together. This is a great way to help glue a show, or series, together. If you can do it effectively, you'll often find your director/producer will love it.

Catalogue Sounds

As Michael Price commented, it's easy to lose track of your sounds, so even with disciplined use of templates, I recommend that you take the time to make a note of sounds you come across that are particularly useful to you. We all have our preferences, so once we find a sound that works, we'll want to go back to it time and again.

Many virtual instruments allow you to mark favorite sounds (and any tweaks you've made to them) or add them to a favorites folder – yet most of us don't use these features! The time lost to searching around for that sound that worked so nicely on some other track you wrote months or years ago can add up. You'll find yourself re-opening sessions and checking myriad possible settings to match them up in your new track. As well as wasting valuable time, this can also disrupt your state of flow when composing.

If your virtual instrument doesn't have the ability to save patches, you may have to use the old-school approach and make a written/computer note of the type of sound and the file path to its location. If you choose to work this way (and if you do, a spreadsheet may be best), be sure to group your sounds by type for quick reference. E.g. Acoustic Guitars (strummed); Acoustic Guitars (solo); Hollow Pads; Bells Pads, etc.

Summary

Creating a palette ahead of time is a tool used by so many professional TV composers for good reason. It will help you establish the instrumentation that works for a show before writing the cues, and will give the episode/series a cohesive sound.

In addition, it will help you during the writing process, as you draw inspiration from this palette. This will help you to write more efficiently and reduce time wasted searching through lists of sounds when you should be writing music!

When you truly have the sound of a show down, and understand what works for its different moods, characters and elements, you'll be surprised at how effortless it can be to create great cues.

Chapter Two – Creating Movement

Music is often used in soundtracks to propel a sequence forward. This is commonly called giving the music "movement" and in this chapter I'll share some ideas on how to create it in a cue. Movement can be dominant and obvious in the music, (such as a percussive, driving feel for a chase sequence), or executed more subtly.

When starting to get ideas for a cue, the first step is to consider the pace of the sequence itself, to discover what tempo works best with the footage. Getting the tempo right to convey the feeling of movement to the viewer is an early building block from which to construct the cue. Mac Quayle sometimes takes this approach:

> *"Sometimes it can just start with a pulse and then I'll write the rest of it on top of that. Other times there will be a melodic or harmonic piece written, then I'll arrange it and add the movement that it needs."*

Movement isn't all about action. Poignant moments may need movement too. One example is a simple, held string note to convey an emotional moment, such as the death of a character. Even for an apparently "static" moment like this, composers will rely on a variety of techniques to keep the scene's forward momentum. I'll explain some of these techniques in a moment. First, it's important to understand the two main categories of movement: Instrument Led Movement and Production Led Movement.

Instrument Led Movement

Instrument Led Movement comes from the instrumental performance itself, whether you're using live musicians or playing the music yourself via samples. One of the most common types of Instrument Led Movement you'll hear in TV soundtracks is the *ostinato*.

An ostinato is a motif or phrase that persistently repeats in the same musical voice.

In TV soundtrack music, an ostinato can work on its own (and cues can sometimes begin this way), but most often will have accompanying chords that move above or below it.

When you start working with an ostinato, it's natural to pick chords that contain the same notes as the phrase, such as Example 2a:

Example 2a:

Alternatively, you might deliberately use clashing passing notes, or adapt your ostinato slightly to accommodate different chord changes. My preference, to prevent the ostinato losing focus, is to use notes as close to the original phrase as possible (neighboring tones), so that it sounds similar to what came before.

In the below example, I've changed the ostinato to fit the harmony in the fourth bar. The ostinato note at the start of bar 4 has moved from F to G to fit the underlying Dm chord.

Example 2b:

Another consideration is the length of the ostinato before it repeats itself. Short ostinatos of one or two beats long, will give you a *relentless* feel at a fast tempo, or a *hypnotic* feel at a slow tempo:

Example 2c:

Example 2d:

You can hear that the intensity of each ostinato backs off a little when the length of the repeated material is extended:

Example 2e:

Example 2f:

Bear in mind that listeners' ears will soon tire of a short ostinato, so you will need to introduce other elements that move and change to keep interest (such as changing the melody, harmony, or moving the ostinato around – which we'll cover in a moment).

Many composers choose an ostinato that anchors itself to the root note of the key of the track. For example, if your main piece is in the key of D minor, your ostinato may contain a lot of D notes, or begin on a D. The ostinato may also function as a pedal note (a constant, repeating note) that ties the harmony and melody together.

Moving an Ostinato Around

One effective technique is to move your ostinato onto different instruments or into a different register. This can signal a gear change in your track, while keeping the material familiar to the listener. You might choose to move the ostinato from the lower strings to the higher strings to give the impression of picking up more energy:

Example 2g:

Or, you can ratchet the intensity down by moving the ostinato from the higher strings to the lower strings and thinning out the textures around it a little:

Example 2h:

Moving the ostinato between instrument groups is a great way of achieving a textural change:

Example 2i:

When using an ostinato, it's important to consider instrumentation and range. In other words, you must allow the other instruments space to breathe. For example, if your ostinato is being played on the low strings, avoid writing the melody or accompanying harmony on low strings too. Avoid other instruments that occupy the same sonic range too. This will allow the ostinato to come through clearly and keep things from sounding muddy.

Popular Ostinato Choices

Below are some examples of common uses of the ostinato. These have been based on certain instruments and registers that seem to be particularly popular in TV soundtrack work. I've also noted the kind of feel they create for the listener. Considerations such as tempo and harmony will hugely affect the resulting feel and therefore the application of the cue, so the examples that follow are to provide you with a guide rather than present hard and fast rules. If any of the "player techniques" are alien to you, these are covered in Chapter Eight under the topic of orchestration.

Low String Ostinato

- Feel: Sinister, menacing, dangerous, ominous.

- Accompanying Harmony: Higher strings; brass.

- Player Technique: Spiccato or staccato.

Example 2j:

High String Ostinato

- Feel: Tension, energy, chase.

- Accompanying Harmony: Lower strings; brass.

- Player Technique: Spiccato or staccato.

Example 2k:

High Woodwind Ostinato

- Feel: Lighter energy.

- Accompanying Harmony: Strings.

- Player Technique: Staccato.

Example 2l:

Piano

- Feel: Mysterious.

- Accompanying Harmony: Strings.

- Player Technique: Legato, soft and rolling feel.

Example 2m:

High Bells

- Feel: Magical, Mystical.

- Accompanying Harmony: Piano, Strings.

- Player Technique: Softly played.

Example 2n:

You'll notice that most of the above examples are in the high or low registers. This is a simple way of leaving sonic space for other instruments to occupy.

Production Led Movement

"A lot of music that I do has an electronic foundation ... so in that world, I'll use all types of things: pulses, arpeggiators, percussion ... whatever feels like it's going to be the right thing. So [the question is], does the movement need to be subtle? Does it need to be more intense, sharper? I'll try all kinds of things to find something that has the right movement." – Mac Quayle

Production Led Movement refers to movement created primarily through the use of production techniques, effects, or from other electronic sources. It's a method of creating movement that doesn't rely on the instrumental performance alone.

Why consider Production Led Movement?

Production Led Movement has some creative advantages that Instrumental Led Movement may not:

- **Creating a modern sound.** Creating movement via production techniques can give a track a more contemporary edge. Be aware, however, that certain sounds/techniques come in and out of fashion. Keep an ear on current soundtracks to make sure you're not using dated sounds/techniques if a modern sound is your goal.

- **Ambiguity.** We know that certain instruments can conjure up certain moods or emotions in themselves. If you want to create movement that doesn't do this, or that is simple, neutral or ambiguous, production led movement is probably the way to achieve it.

The options for creating production led movement with most DAWs are vast, so let's narrow things down to what are considered some of the most effective techniques.

Pulses

Many TV composers use a pulsing element in their cues to great effect. We tend to associate anything that sounds like a ticking clock with the passing of time, or a lack of time. Either way, the listener gets the message that time is important in a particular scene. Similarly, we all tend to recognize music that hints at a heartbeat or pulse as signifying tension, and composers will use this to their advantage. Using an obvious heartbeat sound is generally considered passé these days, but the good news is that audiences are conditioned to pulses in TV music, so you can move away from the obvious.

Many synth and sample plug-ins come with a menu of pulse-like sounds built in. Keep in mind that you'll nearly always need to do some tweaking to make this effect work for your track. Another option is to take a regular sustained sound and create a pulse from it.

A great way to start creating pulses in this way is to open the arpeggiator in your DAW or via the interface of the sample software you've used for the sound. This will chop the sound into smaller chunks (usually 1/8th notes or 1/16th notes), represented by vertical bars. You can raise or lower these bars to make individual chunks louder or quieter.

Example 2o:

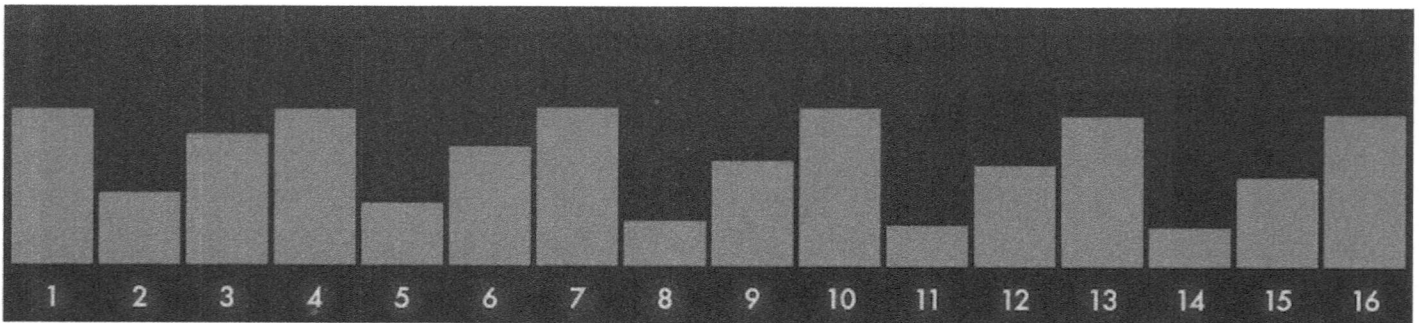

Here are some tricks I like to use when creating pulses for a soundtrack:

- **Avoid complex rhythms in your pulses.** More often than not, you just want to give a little air of tension or the impression of some movement behind other elements of the track. Complex rhythms may pull the listener's focus away and they don't often interact well with other elements.

- **Add just a little delay**. If you need to smooth over the spaces between notes, try adding a delay to the track your pulse is on. Don't go crazy though, start with no delay then fade up the amount of effect, otherwise things can quickly get muddy.

- **Use EQ to carve out room.** I find that pulses work well when they occupy a certain register – either high or low. You may wish to remove some low end from high pulses, or high end from low pulses to carve out room for other instruments. I like to use an EQ with an analyzer function for this so I can see what elements I'm cutting. (We'll cover EQ more in in Chapter Seven).

- **Use a filter.** Another method to get your pulse sounding less intrusive is to run it through a filter, where you can experiment with reducing the cutoff amount. Again, go easy here. Aggressive filtering will sound like your pulse is underwater.

When EQ-ing and filtering pulses to create sonic room, a great tip is to automate the effects, so they gradually increase as other instruments come in. If your pulse sounds great on its own, but less so when other instruments come alongside, make your EQ/filter changes subtle, as the other instruments begin to play, and the listener won't notice.

Moving Textures

Using shifting textures can be a subtle and elegant way to inject a little movement into a track. I find this technique works particularly well for cues that need to sound small and intimate.

What is a moving texture?

This is simply adding extra movement to an otherwise static sound (such as a sustained, held note), or to an element that has little movement to it. Here are some ways you can create moving textures:

Reverse it

Reversing audio (manipulating certain elements in a track so that they sound backwards) can make for effective and interesting textures and can be easier to do than you may think.

The simple way is to see if your sample software plug-in has a "reverse" option. Some plug-ins contain this feature and you can just hit that button and hear a sound processed backwards in real time.

Alternatively, most DAWs can quickly reverse an audio track. If you've recorded something using MIDI, bounce it down as a plain audio track, then right-click on it. This should bring up the option to reverse the audio (if not, look in your menu options). Keep a copy of the original audio to revert back to in case you don't like the reversed version.

What tends to work best when reversed? If your source material has no movement to it whatsoever, then you won't hear a huge difference when it's reversed. Too much movement and it will sound a mess. Ideally, source material with a bit of simple movement to begin with will yield the best results.

Bear in mind note lengths. If you hit a note on beat 2 of a bar and it decays by beat 3, then reversed it will fade from nothing on beat 2 to a high point on beat 3. In other words, consider where you will finish a note to achieve your desired effect.

Example 2p

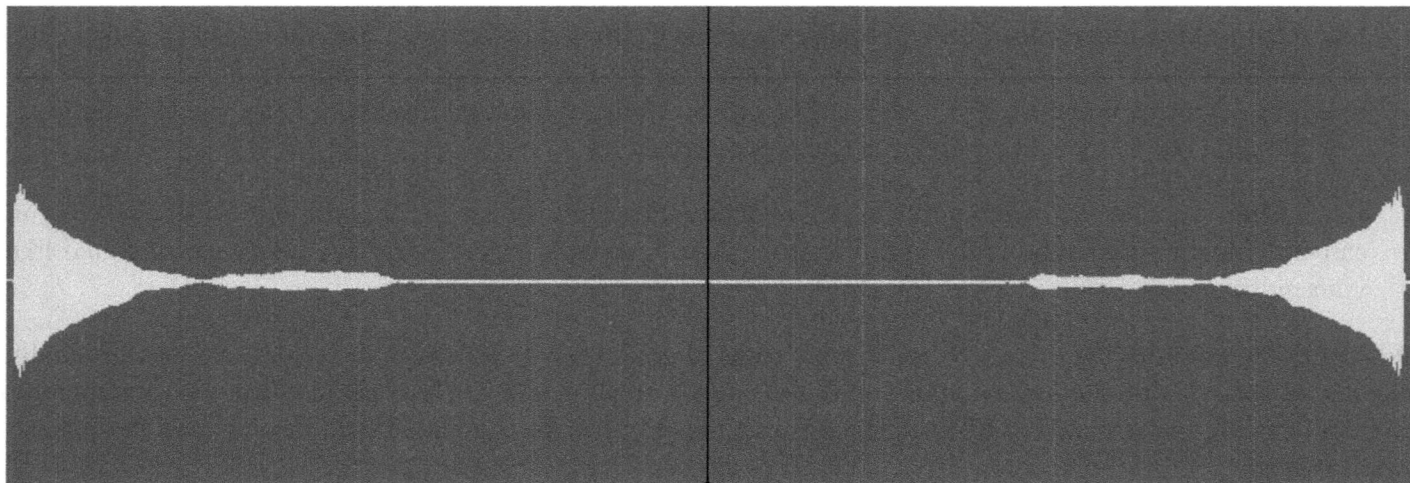

Reversing some elements may give you aggressive peaks and suction effects, and these may need to be smoothed out, which can be achieved with a little filtering or EQ. I tend to blend reversed elements with non-reversed pads or other simple elements, so the reversed material just adds a little movement. It's the combination of the two that creates a pleasing texture.

Here are a few examples of material that seems to work after being reversed, so you can see how much movement is effective:

Example 2q:

Example 2r:

Example 2s:

Delay

Delay may be the Grand Old King of the moving texture, and with good reason. The use of a delay effect allows you to write in an incredibly sparse way, while the delay adds filling to the gaps in an interesting, and often ethereal manner. This can be very useful in TV soundtracks.

As with other effects, start small and subtle and use delay sparingly. Dial up the delay feedback/amount from zero and, little by little, see how it sits alongside other elements in your track.

Subtle delay seems to play well with other effects, so you add a small amount to other effects experiments (such as reversed audio). As always, beware of things becoming muddy. You'll often only want delay on one element.

Let things breathe and if you're not convinced that the delay is doing anything positive, it's usually best that it's not there at all.

Guitar Pedals

Passing sound sources other than guitars through guitar pedals is another TV composer's tool for creating fresh and intriguing sounds. Most DAWs now come with virtual guitar pedals, though I also know several composer friends who swear by the real thing. Either way, these experiments can lead to interesting results, not just for movement purposes but creating all sorts of fascinating sonic angles, as Michael Price points out:

> "I'm a big fan of random stuff. There's a guy in the UK who builds these [effects] boxes with just two or three little chips in, doesn't label them and sells them as one-offs on eBay, and you just take a chance for £100. So, I start a new project and go off into the toy cupboard and find out what real world boxes are going to be fun for this."

Sidechain Compression

Sidechain compression came to mainstream attention through the EDM genre (Electronic Dance Music). It's a way of automating the action of a compressor, telling it that "when instrument A sounds, automatically drop the volume level of instrument B to let A poke through". Instrument B could be one instrument, several, or, as is often the case, *every* other instrument in the mix apart from instrument A.

In EDM, this technique is generally used to allow a kick drum to cut through the mix by cutting the volume of *everything* apart from the kick for a miniscule amount of time, whenever the kick is played. It creates a "suction" effect around the kick drum. It's the same as when a DJ speaks through the mic and the music automatically drops in level, then goes back up afterwards – that's sidechain compression.

How does this help us to create movement in TV music? By using this suction effect in a creative way, you can add some interesting movement to an otherwise static line. You don't have to have a big ol' kick drum playing in order to trigger it!

I could give you a tutorial here on how to route audio through your compressor to create a sidechain, but more often than not you'll just be looking for that classic sidechain "pump" to be added to an element in your track. Instead, I'll point you to an inexpensive plug-in called "Kickstart" by CableGuys and Nicky Romero. This will produce the suction effect much more quickly and easily. Simply drop the Kickstart plugin onto your track, select which type of sidechain effect you'd like, and dial it in via a simple control on the interface. Bingo, interesting movement! By applying the effect to just one instrument/element in your arrangement, rather than everything, you'll achieve a much more subtle and usable effect.

Of course, if you want to learn more about the non-cheating way of rigging up sidechain compression, there are plenty of great tutorials on the Internet!

Combining Instrument Led Movement with Production Led Movement

The combination of electronic and instrumental elements in TV soundtracks is everywhere. Done well, it works brilliantly.

It is, of course, completely possible to combine instrument led movement with production led movement within one element. An example of this could be taking the audio of an instrumental performance that contains rhythmic movement and processing it with effects to add more movement. However, I would be cautious of doing this.

If you've already got one element that moves and you try to create "movement on top of movement", more often than not you'll end up with a mess. Chances are, you're trying to be clever for the sake of it (always a bad idea!) or you need to investigate why your original element is not giving you the movement you want. If it's the latter, try a new idea. If you're convinced more movement is the answer, combining instrument led and production led elements can be interesting e.g. a pulsing synth playing 1/16th notes underneath woodwind. As always, your choices must be governed by the genre and what works for the show.

The Power of Contrast

To end this chapter, I want to share with you an absolutely invaluable tool. It can be applied to creating effective movement, but to a host of other factors in writing soundtrack (or any) music.

The tool is contrast.

In the context of writing music for TV, "contrast" means writing something different from that which has preceded it. The result should be that when the new instrument/element/texture is heard, it sounds completely fresh and therefore has a more significant impact.

I'll give you an example.

Imagine you're scoring a sequence in which a group of criminals are planning a bank robbery. Your director tells you that at the point where the music starts in the scene, the show simply needs a little tension. Shortly after, right after the gang leader says, "Let's do this!" the director wants the music to get going. However, there is still lots of dialogue taking place between the characters, and this will be followed by several more gear changes, so the music mustn't get *too big* here. Let's look at some ways to approach this:

Say that you decide you're going to start with a low, dark, pulsing synth drone for when the cue first comes in. You now want the impact of movement at the next hit point ("Let's do this!"), while keeping the overall texture sparse, to accommodate the dialogue and leave yourself somewhere to go.

Contrast is a great way to do this.

Simple violin 1/8th notes could work, which you can keep in a high register to steer clear of the frequency range of the actors' voices. If you've not used strings up to this point in the sequence, you'll be harnessing *instrumental contrast* – the strings will be a new sound to the listener's ear after the electronic drone (as long as your drone didn't sound too string-like!)

For added contrast, you then might choose to:

1) Stop the movement of the pulsing drone to leave a gap just before the strings come in. This provides contrast between the rhythms.

Example 2t:

2) Experiment with a contrast in rhythm. What if the drone pulsed in 1/4 notes or triplets before the string 1/8th notes? That's a rhythmic contrast.

Example 2u:

3) Stop the drone from continuing under the new violin section, replacing it with low strings if necessary. That's more contrast as a familiar sound is replaced by something totally different.

Example 2v:

Each of these options will add contrast, which in turn will add musical impact. You could stack all of these ideas (illustrated below in Example 2w) or just use one or two, depending on how much impact was deemed appropriate.

Example 2w:

What we've done here is create an effective, noticeable gear change using contrast, but with sparse instrumentation so that the dialogue has room to breathe. Plus, we have left plenty of room to introduce other instruments later, to build up the track from this point.

The effective use of contrast is often the difference between an elegant cue and one that sounds forced, overly dramatic or too busy. Most cues need to develop and grow in some way, propelling the sequence forward and emphasizing the development of the story. When you're new to composing for TV there is a huge temptation to throw more and more instruments at a track in an attempt to make it grow. In fact, this just allows less space for dialogue and sound effects. It can be a key reason why, despite the director genuinely liking your track, it doesn't quite work once it's put to picture.

Simple and effective music is so often the goal within soundtrack writing. Never losing sight of this while developing a track is a true sign of a great soundtrack composer.

Michael Price describes the power of contrast within movement beautifully:

"For certain kinds of scores, the filmmakers are looking for the music to help with pace and energy. So how do you generate that? There's a law of diminishing returns involved, in that the more you put ostinatos on, and the more that you put anything that loops in the background, that sets itself up as the baseline. That means that if you then want to change up a gear, you're already there: you've got nowhere else to go. So, contrast is the technique. Contrast is the aspect that gives you the perception of whatever it is that you need.

Black is at its blackest after you've seen a snowdrift. Quiet is as its quietest after Metallica have finished! So, I think for movement, most composers will know how to make something that moves in an instinctive way, but often the reason that I find a scene isn't working that needs movement, is because I haven't stopped at any point.

So, if you find that something needs to feel like it's moving, and in particular that it's changing gear, you need to stop... then you'll feel the movement when it restarts."

Chapter Three – Chords, Harmony and Temp Music

"I think tension and release and contrast are what I'm always trying to work with all the time, and harmony gives you the judicious selection of the right chord at the right time – the right language to be in. It gives you the range of what you can say in a particular context.

One part is setting yourself a harmonic framework for a project. What kind of show is it? There are certain harmonic progressions in Sherlock that are meaningful in that particular language and are central to the language of Sherlock that I wouldn't use in Unforgotten. They don't sound like Unforgotten. But then what that language has got is extreme ends to it. I know how dissonant I can push something, if the emotion of the scene depends on it, and that won't be the same on Unforgotten as it is for a Horrid Henry The Movie kids type thing!

I'm just working on a psychological thriller at the moment and what's involved in that harmonic language is totally different. But it still has a range. It still has light and shade within the language. It's just that the whole language is shifted up to the dissonant end, but there's still change within that." – Michael Price

It's obviously beyond the scope of this book to explore everything about harmony with regard to TV music. That would take up a whole other book (probably several) and big doorstop things they would be as well. My aim here is to give you as many usable tips as I can that you can implement straight away. My hope is that they'll save you time and give you useful starting points to develop your own ideas.

As Michael Price points out above, giving yourself a harmonic framework can make your life much easier, and ties in with the point made in Chapter One about organizing your palette beforehand. By developing the characteristics of your score (the instruments) and its overall sound (the choice of harmony), finding those aspects that your director loves, the musical essence of the show will be firmly in your grasp.

I'm not saying that every cue in your soundtrack has to conform, but once you've established the overall tone, composing cues will be an altogether easier and more rewarding process. It's worth pointing out that this can be the toughest part of the composing process and most established composers can tell you stories about how they found the perfect elements, chord progression or sounds.

Chord Progressions

Many modern TV scores are production led and this is in no small part due to TV composers coming from a contemporary music background. If production is their strong point, however, harmony is often something that comes less naturally. One of the most frequent questions I hear from producers-turned-composers is which chord progressions should I use and when?

If this is you, below I've listed a selection of chord progressions from different genres that might help you to get "in the zone" of each genre harmonically.

These are by no means the only options, far from it, they are the tip of the iceberg. But if you're short of ideas, they might prove an interesting starting point.

I also want to take this opportunity to point out that nothing will teach you about chord progressions as well as analyzing those used in as many great soundtrack cues as you can lay your hands on.

Example 3A: Dark / suspense chord progression ideas

Bm Cm Am Bm   *Em Cm Gm Bm*   *Am Em Fm Dm*   *Cm Am Ebm F#m*

(i bii vii i)   *(i vi iii v)*   *(i v vi iv)*   *(i vi iii #vi)*

Example 3B: Epic / awe chord progression ideas

Dm Bb F C   *Am Em G D*   *Em G Am Bm*   *Am C Ab F*

(i VI III VII)   *(i v VII IV)*   *(i III iv v)*   *(i III VII VI)*

Example 3C: Emotional / tragedy chord progression ideas

Em G C Am   *Dm F Gm Am*   *Em Am Bm D*   *Fmaj7 Em/G Fmaj7 G9*

(i III VI iv)   *(i III iv v)*   *(i iv v VII)*   *(IV iii IV V)*

Example 3D: Feelgood chord progression ideas

G Am F C   *F Am G C*   *D E F#m A*   *Am7 G Fmaj7 G*

(V vi IV I)   *(IV vi V I)*   *(I II iii V)*   *(vi V IV V)*

Temp Music

"Temp music" is short for temporary music and is the term used by the production team for any music they use whilst making a program. Temp music gives them something to cut to and a feel for what a sequence will be like with a certain musical direction beneath it.

Temp music can come from anywhere: the latest Hollywood blockbuster soundtrack, stock music (also known as library music), a band the editor likes, or tracks you yourself have provided to the production team ahead of time. They're not intended to stay on the show (though sometimes they do) but are for reference only.

Some composers love temp music as it gives them an idea of what the production team think will work in a given scene in terms of feel, tempo, instrumentation and harmony. Exercise caution here though, as they might have picked the track because they liked one or two elements of it, but not others. It's useful to ask what the team did and *didn't* like about a temp track if they feel that your replacement doesn't work.

Other composers hate temp music because the production team can become wed to it. In other words, they get so used to it they have trouble hearing the scene without it. In such a situation, any other music (even if technically it works) will sound wrong to them. Imagine an iconic movie scene, such as when E.T. takes flight on a bicycle and John Williams' theme plays over it. If that music was replaced – even with an alternative written by Williams himself – it would seem strange and we'd want to revert to the original to feel "settled" again.

Changing Temp Music Harmony

If you feel that the chord progression of a piece of temp music is integral in making a scene work, a good strategy is to retain as much of its original "DNA" as possible when replacing it (without simply copying it and getting into legal hot water).

When I set about replacing a temp track that the production team obviously love, the first thing I do is figure out what parts of the progression can be kept, or replaced with a close equivalent. It might be a prominent change between two chords at an important moment that stands out. Or there might be a point at which a change of chord is unusual or unpredictable in its placement.

Always ask the production team to tell you which parts they feel work particularly well. With this information you can decide what must stay and what can be changed.

Practically speaking, how does one set about working with and developing a temp track? Here's the process I use:

1. First, figure out the harmonic framework of the track. What is the chord progression? Is it major or minor? Is there a modal influence (we'll discuss modes in the next chapter) or some altered scale being use that gives it its character?

2. Once you've established the above, write out the diatonic chords of the key or scale used in the track. I find it helps to see the most obvious possible chord options in front of me.

3. Understand the function of the chords before substituting replacements.

Refresher: Chord Functions

Let's refresh ourselves a little with regard to chord functions.

When substituting one chord for another, we need to consider the function of that chord within the progression. We'll divide our categories into three: tonic, dominant and predominant chords.

The I chord is the tonic chord (the chord that describes the key). Chords that have a dominant function move easily to the I chord, and most strongly the V chord. Predominant chords are those that move easily to dominant chords.

Tonic Chords

The tonic chord serves as "home". The I chord is the prime example of creating the "home" sound, but is not the only diatonic chord that can achieve this feeling. For example, the vi chord is a common substitute for the I. If we had the progression set out in Example 3e:

Example 3e:

G C D G

(I IV V I)

We might choose to end it with the vi chord, which would make it:

Example 3f:

G C D Em

(I IV V I)

It's less strong than the I chord, but a perfectly viable option. Returning to the IV chord (C major) is another option.

Dominant Chords

Dominant chords move easily to tonic chords and the most common option is the V chord. In our example in the key of G Major, that would be a D7 chord.

The favored option is the V chord, but an alternative is the iii chord (Bm):

Example 3g:

G C Bm G

(I IV iii I)

The vii (Fdim) is also an option:

Example 3h:

G C Fdim G

(I IV vii I)

Predominant Chords

Predominant chords are chords that want to move to the dominant chord. The most obvious is the IV chord. In the key of G Major that would be the C major chord. However, there are other options. The favored option is the IV chord, but you may also use the ii chord (Am).

Example 3i:

G Am D G

(I ii V I)

The vi chord (Em) is another choice.

Example 3j:

G Em C G

(I vi V I)

Hopefully you'll see that mixing and matching these options helps retain the essence of the original progression, but provides a useful launchpad from which you can explore its harmonic possibilities.

Further Concepts

Here are some other concepts you might want to consider when moving your music away from the temp, or just include in your writing in general.

Altering the beat of chord changes

Changing the beat on which a chord falls (as well as changing the chord itself) is a nice way of moving further away from the temp.

The challenge is to do this tastefully if the original chord changes are not syncopated. The chords of the temp music may change every bar and land on the first beat each time. In which case, doing any other than altering the harmony might detract from the character of the piece. However, occasionally changing chord on beat 3 might create enough differentiation and interest.

If the original chords are already quite syncopated, you'll have many more options to experiment with that won't take away from the feel of the track too much.

Altering bass notes

Altering bass notes can be a subtle yet powerful change. This may be as simple as using the third of a chord as the bass note instead of the root. You could, for instance play G/B to C, instead of just playing G to C. Alternatively, instead of playing a chord inversion, you could add a bass note that results in a different chord sound. Put an F bass against a C major chord and you now have Fmaj7. That might be too much of a change, so experiment to see what resonates with the temp track and what moves too far away from it.

Different keys take you to different places

I think it's good practice to change the key of a cue you're writing to make it different from the temp. You may initially find that the chord progression doesn't sound quite right in another key, because each key has its own distinct sound. But changing key can be a great source of inspiration. You'll find yourself playing things in one key that you might not do in another.

Use this to your advantage and get used to the sound of your new key. Look to see where you could change the temp progression to make it sound better in the new key. This exercise in itself can open up new options that move you away from the temp track.

Suspensions

Suspensions are commonly heard in TV soundtrack harmony and are great for adding a tense, heart-wrenching or unresolved feel. For those new to this idea, it means sustaining (or "suspending") one note from a chord so that it bleeds into the next. The sustained note is normally dissonant and clashes with the new chord, but then resolves to a chord tone.

In traditional western classical music you need to "prepare" a suspension. This means you hear it in the first chord before the clash occurs, then you resolve it. However, you'll hear such suspensions in film and TV soundtracks without any preparation. Composers will just jump in with this delicious clash without warning. By all means take this approach if it works better for you!

Here are the four most common suspensions along with their resolutions, labelled as intervals above the bass note:

Example 3k:

Michael Price has this advice about being creative with tension:

"I do a show called Unforgotten – it's a nice detective show. The harmonic language of it is quite classical: lots of 4-3 suspensions, lots of pedal notes, or inverted pedal notes – where you're holding something across the top and the chords change underneath.

The heart of what makes that show sound like it does is the combination of instrument choices – of having a high cello playing over the top of lower strings. But also harmonically, a lot of the time I'm using the harmonic tension that comes from having chords that are constantly suspended across the bar line all the time. I'm always interested in finding that semitone clash, not by jumping straight into it, but by setting it up a little before so that the chord underneath moves to it, finds that point of tension and then chooses to release or not."

Two Harmonic Framework Examples

To end this chapter, here are two short soundbites from Mac Quayle and Michael Price about techniques they used to create a harmonic signature for shows they've worked on.

American Horror Story: Moving Minor Chords In Minor Third Intervals

"In the darker things that I work on, like American Horror Story, a favorite harmonic thing for me is moving minor chords around in minor third intervals. There's a creepy unsettling sound, also a classic horror sound where you take an A Minor, then move it up to C Minor and then move that up to Eb Minor. It does some creepy things which I like. That's one of the more go-to things for me." –Mac Quayle

The Sherlock Sound: Major/Minor Chord Four

"For part of the musical language for Sherlock that David Arnold and I did together, a lot of the harmony comes from two or three key themes, which are more harmonic than melodic really. The opening title sequence and the main hero theme has got a thing about major/minor chord four.

So, if you are in D minor, do you play G major or do you play G minor? Because in both the title sequence and in that theme, they've both got major or minor chord fours. So if you substitute them, or move from one to the other, it sounds "Sherlock-y" straight away. Whereas I wouldn't do that change in Unforgotten, it wouldn't feel like part of the language.

There's something about changing from a major chord to a minor chord, or vice versa, that has quite a dramatic quality to it – quite a theatrical change from light to dark, or dark to light, that sits within that [Sherlock] language, where it doesn't quite sit in the same way in a more classical sounding score, or whatever the modal language I use in Unforgotten." –Michael Price

Chapter Four – Modes

"It took me a while to get to this place, but these days I'm just obsessed with the emotional connection with the different tones in a mode, and not at all interested in the technical, theoretical sense ... Hopefully that's because at some level I've absorbed some of the technical information and can let it go now!" – Michael Price

I love this quote that Michael gave when I interviewed him. It's important that each tool, tip, trick, idea or technique you learn from this book, first and foremost, *serves the project* and scene you are writing for. Remember our mantra from Chapter One:

You are first and foremost part of the storytelling team, you just happen to be working with music.

As we explore modes and altered scales (don't be intimidated by that term if it's new to you, all will be revealed!) you'll find that they give you some strong flavors and emotions to play with in your compositions. Have fun and experiment with them – it's great to have them in your compositional arsenal – but make sure the scene requires that strong emotion and you're not trying to crowbar it in to be clever.

Modes and the Flavors They Bring

A mode is simply a scale. Just as the Major and Minor scales are associated with happy and sad moods respectively, modes expand these options and give other scale options that can create different moods. We are interested in them from a TV scoring perspective because of these additional emotions they suggest, to broaden our harmonic/melodic palette.

Just as emphasizing the flattened third note in a minor chord reinforces the strong minor sound, modes have their own pressure points and can be "leant on" in order to emphasize their unique character. It's good to know where in a mode its strongest flavor is located and use this when composing for a scene.

Below is each mode written out with a C note as its root – first as a scale, then as chords. I've noted which intervals you can stress to bring out the unique flavor of the mode, and also the moods that the mode tends to conjure up. When composing, you might decide to base your framework around one particular mode and the chords it generates when harmonized.

Ionian Mode

The Ionian mode is exactly the same as the major scale.

Mood: Bright, happy, uplifting.

Example 4a:

The chords made up from the Ionian mode:

Example 4b:

Dorian Mode

The Dorian mode gets it's character from the dark/sad flavor of its minor 3rd, but also the unexpected brightness of its major 6th. Points of tension you may wish to exploit are created between the 2nd and the flattened 3rd intervals, the 6th and the flattened 7th, and the flattened 3rd and the 6th.

This mode is often used in Funk, Blues and Jazz music. Dorian based tracks include *So What* by Miles Davis, *Eleanor Rigby* by The Beatles and *Purple Haze* by Jimi Hendrix.

Mood: Melancholy, but with a surprising brightness (via the major 6th).

Example 4c:

The chords made up from the Dorian mode:

Example 4d:

Dm	Em	F	G	Am	Bdim	C	Dm
i	ii	III	IV	v	vi	VII	i
min	min	Maj	Maj	min	dim	Maj	min

Phrygian Mode

The Phrygian mode is the only mode to have a flattened 2nd and a natural 5th. You may wish to exploit the inherent darkness created by the minor 2nd interval between the root note and the flattened second, and again between the natural 5th and the minor 6th.

I've heard this mode referred to as the Spanish Gypsy scale before, as it resembles the sound of Flamenco music. Interestingly, if you play the Phrygian mode but choose to raise 3rd to a major 3rd instead of a minor 3rd, you get a very "eastern" sound.

Mood: Spanish, folk, medieval. Can be eastern or Arabic sounding if you replace the minor 3rd with a major 3rd.

Example 4e:

The chords made up from the Phrygian mode:

Example 4f:

Em	F	G	Am	Bdim	C	Dm	Em
i	II	III	iv	v	VI	vii	i
min	Maj	Maj	min	dim	Maj	min	min

Lydian Mode

The Lydian mode is a major scale with a sharpened 4th. Lean on that sharpened fourth, as this gives the mode its color. Many composers like to highlight the natural 5th, then the sharpened 4th, so you can really pick it out.

The Lydian mode is all over film and TV music. You'll hear it repeatedly in the iconic theme for *The Simpsons* where it lends a quirky feel to the piece. It also features in the *Back To The Future* theme, as well as in John Williams' compositions in films such as *E.T.* and *Jurassic Park*. It always seems to add a little magic to proceedings, whether that be in a mystical or majestic way.

Mood: Magical; mystical; wonderment.

Example 4g:

The chords made up from the Lydian mode:

Example 4h:

F	G	Am	Bdim	C	Dm	Em	F
I	II	iii	iv	V	vi	vii	I
Maj	Maj	min	dim	Maj	min	min	Maj

Mixolydian Mode

The Mixolydian mode is a major scale but with a flattened 7th. That flattened 7th is the color note of this mode and can give a really interesting and unexpected aspect to melodic lines and chords made up from this mode.

You'll hear the Mixolydian mode a lot in Rock music, but you can also add a slightly uplifting aspect to your melodies when you incorporate that all important flattened 7th.

Mood: Slightly uplifting; Rock/Pop.

Example 4i:

The chords made up from the Mixolydian mode:

Example 4j:

Aeolian

The Aeolian mode is also referred to as the Natural Minor scale. The intervals that make up it's characteristic sound are it's flattened 3rd, flattened 6th and flattened 7th. Some composers also really like to exploit the tritone interval between the 2nd interval and the 6th interval of this mode.

Mood: Sad; lonely; introspective.

Example 4k:

The chords made up from the Aeolian mode:

Example 4l:

Locrian

I've saved the weirdest for last! The Locrian mode has a minor sound created by flattening both the 3rd and the 6th, but also the 2nd, 5th and 7th too!

The Locrian mode has an unfinished sound to it that almost resists being resolved. To that extent, it always reminds me of the sound that might be associated with an instrumental cadenza.

Mood: Tense and uneasy; unresolved; cadenza-like.

Example 4m:

The chords made up from the Locrian mode:

Example 4n:

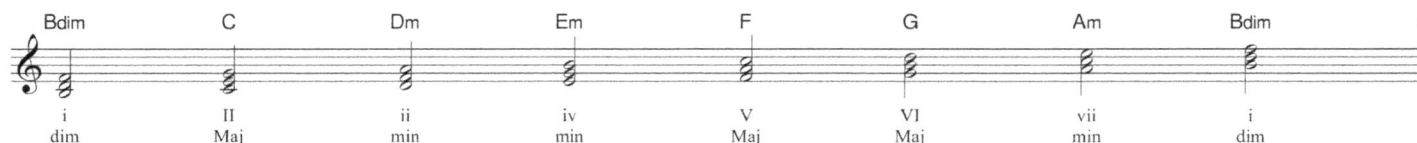

Lydian Dominant

If scales and modes are just different combinations of tones and semitones, then we don't have to stop at the above examples. It's possible to experiment with these scales to come up with new, altered scales. For example, I've heard the Lydian mode be given a flattened seventh and referred to as "The Cartoon Scale":

Example 4o:

That's a pretty useful tool to discover if you're writing that style of cartoon music!

Here are its resulting chord triads, this time written in C:

Example 4p:

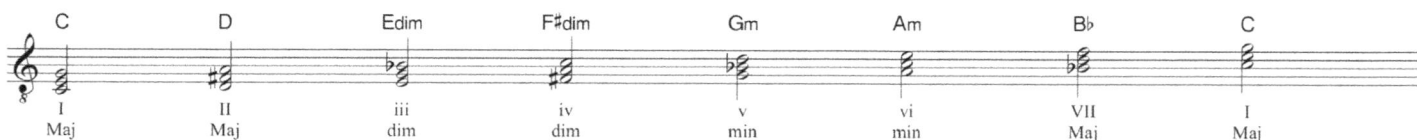

Pentatonic Scales

We're all familiar with the pentatonic scale (easily remembered by playing all black notes on the piano). Here it is in the key of C:

Example 4q:

The following example is also a five-note scale, but with a much more major quality:

Example 4r:

Don't get too bogged down by terminology here – feel free to experiment. The idea is to illustrate that there are many emotions to be tapped into, apart from those offered by the standard Major and Minor scales.

Absorbing Modal Flavors

The more you work with the modes, the more you'll absorb the unique flavor of each one and become adept at highlighting its unique sound. As you play and experiment, you'll find these sounds seeping into your compositions when appropriate. In time, this will become automatic. Mac Quayle says,

> *"I don't sit down and think: 'This is going to be a Dorian mode thing.' It's just kind of a feel. I'll write the initial handful of cues and establish the feel and the sound of the project, then the mode just sort of comes out of that. Then anything I write from that point forward, it either feels like it fits with the sound, or it doesn't.*
>
> *After the fact, I could go back and analyze and see what mode I was in, but I don't do it consciously, it's just a feel."*

Always Serve The Scene

I make no apologies for repeating this important point, but remember the story comes first! Don't use modes for the sake of it or to try and be clever. Used appropriately, however, the colors arising from apt mode/scales choices can inject some fantastic character into your score.

"If you're being super honest emotionally and listening to what you're doing as an audience member, or as a producer, or somebody who isn't listening as a musician, then maybe some of the modes that have a flat second in or flat sixth, and have a specific flavor to them ... you have to listen to them and ask, 'Is this serving the emotional need of the scene right now?'

That's whether or not it's smart, or reminds you of John Coltrane ... basically, if there's a muso [musician] reason to do something, but not a film reason to do it, then NO!

But those are all colors that we've got in our palette. Pulled out at the right time they can be incredibly effective, but it's always got to be to serve the drama.

There's a cue early on, at the end of the second series of Sherlock, called 'Blood On The Pavement' which is after Sherlock has jumped off the rooftop and is, according to John Watson's point of view, dead. Blood coming out of him on the pavement.

The harmony there is fully chromatic, with a strange sense of where any kind of root is at all. A cue like that at any other point in the series would just seem weird and gratuitous. But the direction suggests it: the camera starts to move round and Watson is almost hallucinating... or is he... and at that point, in that scene, at that particular climactic, pivotal, surreal moment, that harmony is absolutely justified.

So context is everything." –Michael Price

Chapter Five – Melody and Motifs

In this chapter we'll explore the role of melody in a TV score and consider how to approach melodic ideas. We'll consider when the use of a melody can be most effective and what purpose it serves within a score. Firstly though, some clarifications.

The Difference Between a Theme, a Melody and a Motif

We'll be referring to *themes*, *melodies* and *motifs* as we move forward. I don't want to bog you down with terminology, but broadly speaking:

- A *theme* is a type of long-form melody that is associated with a certain situation or character in a show. For example, the opening titles.

- A *melody* (again, long-form) can occur at various places during a TV show or film, but might not be the show's main theme. This can be used to associate with a particular situation, without being tied to a specific character.

- A melodic *motif* is a smaller idea (short-form) and can be just a few notes.

In reality, TV shows may contain of combination of the above, comprising long-form melodies and short motifs. The title theme may occur at the beginning and end of a show, for instance, and shorter motifs be heard throughout. The motifs may contain parts of the main theme, or be totally different.

Motifs can work well to express a recurring idea. If we played a short, four-note motif every time the character Bob showed up on screen, we could call that "Bob's theme". I wouldn't necessarily disagree with that, but let's leave those debates to the academics! In a nutshell:

Melody = Longer melodic phrases

Motif = Short fragments

The Move Away From The Big Melodic Approach

Over the last couple of decades, TV composers have largely moved away from composing at their piano or with a guitar, and begun writing in front of their DAWs. This has resulted in tracks that are much more production led, rather than melody led. Those readers who grew up with '80s shows such as *The A-Team*, *Knight Rider* and *Dallas* (as well as the soap operas your parents used to watch) can probably still recall and sing those big, strong themes.

Some modern shows contain equally memorable themes (such as *The Simpsons*). Others open with songs (*Family Guy*). Some opening sequences are production led, with only a small nod to a melody (such as *E.R.* in the '90s), or are essentially just motifs themselves (such as *Breaking Bad*).

The production led approach has led to scores with less obvious melodic content that often feel more "modern". I don't think this is necessarily by design, or that it's good or bad – it's just the way things have evolved. As Michael Price comments,

> *"Producers or listeners can associate 'tunes' with a score being old fashioned. When somebody says that, it tends to mean that there's a sense of the music becoming front and center, and almost demanding your attention for the period of time that a longer theme plays out. And because that was a technique that was used a lot in films from the forties, fifties and sixties, some people associate longer melodies with something that is of that more traditional scoring variety.*
>
> *I don't think that's necessarily true at all. I think it again depends on context."*

Opening Sequences

The start of a show is usually where, if at all, a long form melody or theme can be established.

That said, in most of the documentaries I've scored, the narrator has spoken over the opening sequence leading up to the titles (known as the *Pre-titles*, which usually end with a "title card" i.e. when the name of the show is displayed on the screen).

The pre-titles are very important for documentary work and you'll find that the production team want to work with you closely to set the tone for the show perfectly. This is for good reason: these fifty to ninety seconds will often be where a viewer decides whether or not to invest the next hour of their time watching the show. As such, it's often about creating excitement, tension, or some kind of heightened emotional state. Much like a film trailer, the footage shows you a montage of some of the most exciting highlights of what you're about to see.

Sometimes the production team have wanted me to write a track with no theme for the pre-titles music, since it will be dialogue heavy. In other cases – most often when it's a series rather than a one-off documentary – they do want a series theme stated. When this is the case, I've often been given a rough-cut of the pre-titles with a rough voiceover recorded on it. The final voiceover goes on after all the music has been dubbed onto the show, so this is never the actual narrator at this stage, but the editor or director. This gives you a good idea of what's required and the placement of the voiceover.

I don't try to weave melodic material purposefully in-between narration because that would sound too contrived. I use the script and accompanying images to define any high points in the scene. I'm aware of avoiding faster moving melodic ideas during dialogue-heavy moments, saving them for the quieter moments.

The big takeaway here is to let things breathe as much as possible and take an "if in doubt, strip it out" approach. If there is no dialogue for the opening sequence, then of course you can have free reign to be creative.

Why Have Melodies at All?

This question is not as crazy as it seems in the context of TV scoring.

Remove the melody from your favorite pop track and you're left with a distinctly less satisfying experience, but a large percentage of TV music is underscore. In the TV environment, a melody – even a simple motif – can distract when dialogue is occurring and pull the viewer's attention away – and that's the last thing a soundtrack should do.

Used effectively, melodies and motifs are an amazing tool at your disposal which give you the ability to create a bond between the viewer and a certain character, situation, location or emotion. Once you've achieved that, you have an immensely powerful tool for storytelling. Once a melody is absorbed into the viewer's consciousness, you can conjure up that association whenever you like, even if nothing on screen suggests it. I think this is one of the most exciting dimensions music can add to production: to make a viewer feel something and they don't even know why.

"Melody is often about memory. And that's memory for the audience. The reason why we use motifs and melodies is to have something which, early on in the film or show, you attach to a particular character or, more interestingly I think, to a particular idea." – Michael Price

Character Themes

"Sometimes the producers will request: 'We want a theme for this character.' Other times it will happen organically: It will come out of writing a cue.

So I'll write a cue and in that cue there'll be a melody, and though none of us were necessarily thinking, 'This is the theme for this character', it works so well that it just follows the character around through the project.

The producers tend to be a little bit loose with it: This one theme might follow the character around for most of the series, but then it feels right to them to put it in another situation with a different character and they'll do that. We're certainly not following this strict thematic approach where each character has his own melody and that's the only way we can use that melody. It's a bit more loose." – Mac Quayle

If you're writing a theme for a character, the chances are it'll either be a motif, or a theme that is easily broken down into smaller sections that you can use as a motif. This allows for greater flexibility later, when you want the motif to fit into smaller places in the show, and to do so elegantly, without being too obvious or pulling away the viewer's attention.

Character themes can be used to remind viewers of one character, even when they're not on screen. If the wife of nice guy "Andrew" is having an affair, playing the melodic motif associated with Andrew during a scene featuring only his wife and her lover will most likely make the audience feel uncomfortable. It would remind viewers of his demeanor and reinforce her cheating nature.

Occasionally, the theme of a show will double as the main character's theme. This is usually most appropriate when a show revolves around that one character.

"One interesting example is the Bond theme at the end of Casino Royale. In David Arnold's amazing score to this film, he doesn't play the Bond theme until right at the end. It's the closing sequence, really.

Because Casino Royale was a reboot – like an origins story for Bond – then at that point he wasn't Bond [as we know him], until right at the end, where there's an iconic shot of him standing with his foot on Mr White, I think the character is. All of a sudden David does this amazing arrangement of the theme that makes you go, 'Ah, and now he's Bond!'" – Michael Price

Concept Themes

"A character theme would be 'See Hobbit: Play Hobbit!'

A concept theme is much more interesting I think. If you've got a theme or a motif which is about hope, or love, or redemption, or coming through out of adversity… then you can apply that theme to various characters or situations.

If the theme or motif is memorable enough for an audience member to then connect one situation with another situation, then you've achieved something through the use of music that isn't possible through any of the other forms." – Michael Price

The concepts you could choose for a theme are almost endless. Here are a couple of popular angles to consider:

- **Overarching Story or Emotions.** One of the first possibilities to consider is to draw on one facet of the overarching story, or focus on a particular emotion. This can be especially interesting if this facet of the story isn't being told on screen. If, for instance, the show is predominantly a thriller with a love story woven in, you could experiment with the latter, while the show emphasizes the former. Keep in mind that the most effective scores try to steer clear of reiterating what is obvious in the footage.

- **Location and Era.** You could bleed just a little information about a location and/or era into the instrumental and scale/modal choices of your theme. This would be most interesting and effective when not blatantly connected to what's happening on screen. Yes, there will be times where you score a program and the location changes to, say, India, so the director asks you for something with an Indian feel. Aside from instances like this, make sure any unique choices have a story-driven concept behind them (as discussed in Chapter One's section, The Constant Quest For New and Fresh).

"My favorite example was in the film Love Actually, that I was the music editor for. In Craig Armstrong's beautiful score for that there is a 'Green Shoots' theme, as they called it. If you go back and look at Love Actually, whenever somebody falls in love, there's a little clarinet motif. It's four or six bars maybe: not that long. The first time you hear it you go, 'That's kind of cute.' But each time, because it's memorable enough, you smile and there's an extra layer of the joke because it's like, even the kids are falling in love now!" –Michael Price

Playing with Point of View

Whether writing character themes or concept themes, altering the point of view can be a fascinating experiment. The choice of music for a particular scene will create a particular atmosphere and can recall or foreshadow different aspects of the narrative. So what if you alter this from the expected direction? What if the theme originates from the point of view of a less obvious character? Does this character know something the audience doesn't? What about creating the impression that the audience knows something the characters don't? Would tricking the audience into believing something now, give a better payoff down the line when the truth is revealed?

The possibilities are almost endless, just make sure you stay true to serving the story as effectively as you can.

Writing a Great Melody

"So I think the absolute length of a motif or melody is immaterial in that it needs to function. If you want to play it again and have somebody remember it, it has to have enough 'information' in it for it to be memorable. That could be sixteen bars or three notes. And it's like salt building up on the hull of a ship: The longer you live with a tune, the more memories you ascribe to it, the more resonant it is when you play it at a particular time.

So I think they [melody and motifs] are incredibly important, but [also] for composers to find their language for each project and how the use of melodies are going to work within that." – Michael Price

There's a reason why I have talked a great deal about story, characters and concepts so far, and am only now addressing the considerations of writing the music itself. Once you have decided the *purpose* of your melody, theme or motif, only then should you start thinking about what it will be musically. Trust me, it will save you time in the long run and help you void writing great melodies that just don't work for the show.

The title of this section, "Writing a Great Melody", is therefore all about composing the *right melody* for the show, concept or character – not just a pleasing tune.

Getting Inspired

If the perfect tune leaps into your brain while you're walking down the road or in the shower, fantastic! However, if it doesn't you'll most probably need to give the creativity a little nudge. It's likely you'll be working to a strict deadline, unless you're able to come up with ideas way ahead of time.

Once you've established the purpose of your theme, explore what instrument choices feel right. Writing ideas on that instrument (or with the relevant samples loaded), is a good start. Just be open to trying different options, should things move forward with that choice.

If no obvious instrument choices spring to mind to nudge inspiration, you might choose to experiment with some of the scale and mode combinations in the last chapter. Playing around with the relationships between certain tones that are inherently light or dark, depending on your goal, can give birth to some relevant musical ideas.

Even how you approach tones in a given mode can give drastically different sounding results. For example, say you want to experiment with the Lydian mode. Approaching the raised fourth lyrically from the happy major third like this…

Example 5a:

…will give you a different feel than going approaching it directly from the root note:

Example 5b:

Consider the tempo too, of course. Are you looking for something spritely? Something steady or lumbering? Something dreamy, with no sense of time at all?

Would it be useful to factor in time signature ahead of time? Perhaps a 6/8 feel may give a softer, rolling feel. Would an odd time signature with an unsettling feel be more appropriate to the aim of the theme?

Can you see how every musical decision I'm making is based on what purpose the melody/motif will fulfill within the story? Never lose sight of that goal in the decisions you make.

Mixing up these different aspects can sometimes give you a multi-faceted solution that works perfectly. It may be that the unsettled feel of an odd time signature, coupled with a playful choice of melody notes reflects the different aspects of the show/character perfectly!

Question and Answer, Tension and Release

One effective approach when writing melodies is to create a "question and answer" structure. This can be done in a number of ways. One long form way could be an "a b a c" structure, as in Example 5c.

Example 5c:

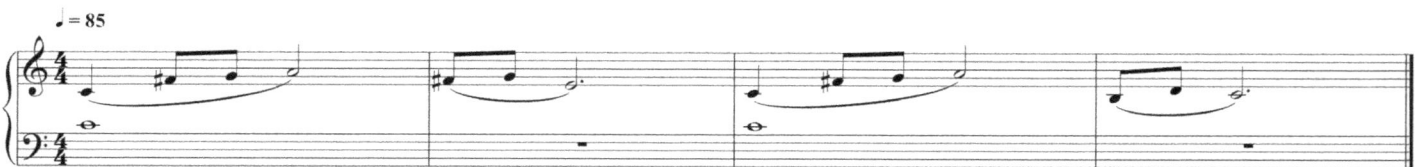

One of the advantages of this approach for a TV soundtrack is that you can use a portion of a melody at a later stage to interesting effect. In other words, you could use the first part only – asking the question, but not answering it. Or you could use just the answer part of the melody at a certain point in the show where the plot reaches a resolution. Depending on how you associate a melody over the course of a production, the question and answer device can be an interesting storytelling tool.

Similarly, you could approach this concept by seeing the two sections as tension and release. Here's a motif example of this.

Example 5d:

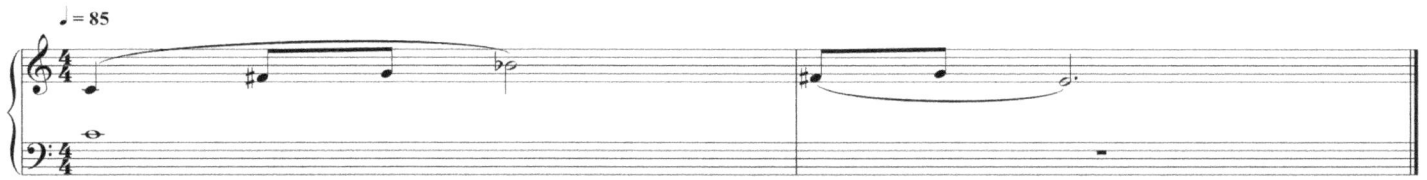

Rising and Falling

Don't underestimate the associations people have with melodies that rise versus melodies that fall.

I was working on one documentary where the director automatically interpreted any rising melodic idea as hopeful, optimistic and positive, and any falling melodies as sad, contemplative and reflective. Whether everyone else on the production team did was debatable – and I'm not trying to establish a rule here – but since then the effect of rising and falling melodies is always in the back of my mind when writing melodies.

Sometimes, I'll have a melody that I'm 80% happy with and I'll tinker around with it to see if moving the odd note here and there will improve things. Maybe things need to be added or taken away? This is often the point at which I'll add ascending or descending phrases to emphasize what I'm trying to achieve.

Another useful approach is to alter your melody slightly to ascend or descend, depending on the context of a scene.

Now let's discuss a critical stage many composers overlook: stress-testing your theme.

Stress Test Your Theme

So you've written a theme that you're happy with. Excellent! It's time to stress test it. What does this mean? It's time to put it through its paces to see if it will stand up to other aspects and situations the show might demand of it. It's important to do this right after you think you've nailed your theme, as it can make the difference between smooth sailing and choppy waters ahead.

Let me give you an example.

For several of the nature and natural history documentaries I've scored, the directors have loved having a theme that we can refer back to. This has taken the form of an overall series theme, which has served as the pre-titles to each show, but then resurfaced at various points throughout each episode. Used in this way, it has an overarching quality that can make a sequence feel like it belongs to the same world as other parts of the show. It can also help give viewers that feeling of "home" within each sequence. A theme like this can serve to tie sections of the program together, plus, to be honest, sometimes the director just likes me throwing it in there from time to time! (Just don't overdo it!)

In the early days, I'd focus on writing a great theme for the pre-titles sequence. I remember one time writing a melody, the movement of which had some powerful moments emphasizing its minor-sounding flavor. When backed up with some powerful orchestration (lots of brass, plenty of strings and some driving percussion) it seemed to be doing a great job as a pre-titles contender, and the producers were happy for me to explore it further.

Only when I came to quote this theme in other parts of the show did its limitations dawn on me. There were scenes that were tender, emotional and moving. My theme, with its stark minor sounding movements, was completely the wrong kind of thing for those moments. When I tried to move individual notes to make these minor movements into major intervals, it just sounded odd and too far removed from the main theme. When I tried to change the chords under the melody – in the hope of inferring less of a minor emphasis – I was forced into using a small set of chord changes that simply didn't work.

I was hitting brick walls at every turn.

Luckily, all this happened at the beginning of the schedule when time was on our side, plus the producers were open to other ideas for the pre-titles theme (perhaps a polite way of saying it wasn't as good as I thought it was!) So we tried other themes and eventually found something that fit the bill. (As a side note, I've done projects where I've created over fifteen different themes and their subsequent mock-ups before we've found the right one. Don't worry if you don't nail it straight away!)

After this experience, I always stress test my theme ideas. I do this by producing four or five versions of the theme in different guises: reflective and moving, upbeat and fun, inquisitive, the warm finale… you get the idea. You can make little changes here and there to do this, but it should always sound like your theme. You'll realize pretty quickly if you're hitting a bunch of brick walls as I was!

Sometimes, if production hasn't started yet and I'm going backwards and forwards with the team on ideas for the theme, I'll actually send them these little stress test sketches (in other words, 20-30 second samples), once we feel we're closing in on what our theme might be.

Keep in mind that it is the main theme to a show that needs extensive stress testing. You don't need to stress test a one-off theme for a specific scene in the show if you won't need to adapt it for other applications.

Here are a few questions you might find it useful to ask yourself when you're stress testing your theme:

- Does it work on a small scale (with sparse instrumentation)?

- Does it work on a large scale (with a full orchestra, for example)?

- Does it work at a different tempo?

- Is it only good at conveying one emotion (sad/happy/tense)?

- Can it fit over alternative chord progressions easily?

- Does it work on different instruments in your palette?

- Can sections be easily extracted to form self-contained motifs that are still recognizable?

Again, your theme doesn't have to adhere to all of these rules, but if you're hitting brick walls in stress testing, you might be making life harder for yourself later on.

Melodic Transformation

"The melodies I write tend to be pretty short. Like a motif. They tend to be simple, just like a few notes, something direct.

Then I'll do some of the normal things you might do with it: I'll let it develop a little, I'll throw it around different instruments, slow it down, speed it up, maybe make an ostinato out of the melody... all the things that can make use of that sequence of notes.

In so many of the programs that I've worked on it's been short, simple melodies." – Mac Quayle

Once you have a melody or motif that seems to be working for you, and you've stress tested it for application, there are a number of ways you can transform the melody.

By "transform" I mean either to change it to maintain interest, or alter it to make it appropriate for other situations and the host of challenges scoring a show can bring up. In this section I'll be talking about ways to transform a melody without taking it so far from the original that you may as well be writing new material.

Usually, you will want to find ways of transforming a melody that will retain enough of its DNA to make it still somewhat recognizable. At one end of the spectrum is making small changes to a melody so that it sounds much like the original, to radical changes, so that it bears only a vague resemblance to its former self. The latter approach has its place and can be an interesting tool to use in a score, and for audiences to experience.

Another, more practical, application of melodic transformation is to extend a short idea to fit a longer sequence by developing the melody. This can save a great deal of time when you're writing to a deadline. Stretching out your material like this – even in adventurous ways that the audience won't directly associate with the original theme – can often lead to music that still sounds united with your source material.

The examples that follow show how far away from your original material these transformations can take your listener. However, this is also governed by how far you push each concept!

Chromatic Inflection

Perceived change from original material: Slight

This form of melodic transformation simply refers to taking a note from the melody and altering it up or down to make it more chromatic than diatonic. You might want to do this to alter the melody to perhaps add some tension or mystery. Another reason could be to make the melody fit better with a change in harmony that you want to make. This first example…

Example 5e:

…might become:

Example 5f:

Adding and Subtracting

Perceived change from original material: Slight to considerable

Adding to or removing notes from your melody can produce interesting results. Obvious uses are adding momentum to an existing melody, or thinning it out so that it alludes less obviously to the original.

Example 5g:

Example 5h:

Example 5i:

Retrograde

Perceived change from original material: Considerable to extreme.

Retrograde means to reverse the order of the melody's notes and can be a pretty extreme change. Such a technique can be more useful to quickly create new, but related, material without directly referencing your main theme. Bear in mind that you can apply this reversal technique to a chord progression as well as a melody.

An exact retrograde would mean using the pitches and rhythms in reverse. So this melody…

Example 5j:

…would become:

Example 5k:

Alternatively, you could experiment with keeping the notes the same but reversing the rhythm, or keeping the rhythm the same and reversing the notes.

If we take Example 5J's melody, keep the pitches the same, but reverse the rhythms we get:

Example 5l:

If we take Example 5j's melody, keep the rhythms the same, but reverse the pitches we get:

Example 5m:

Inversion

Perceived change from original material: Considerable to extreme

Another way to make a radical change is to invert or mirror the original tune. The original moves up a minor second and the inverted form moves down a minor second. Again, this technique is more useful for generating new material.

Example 5n:

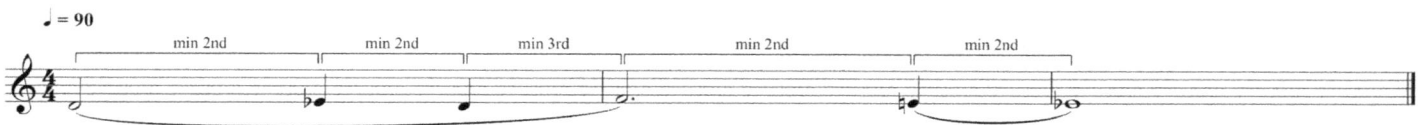

The exact inversion of Example 5n would be:

Example 5o:

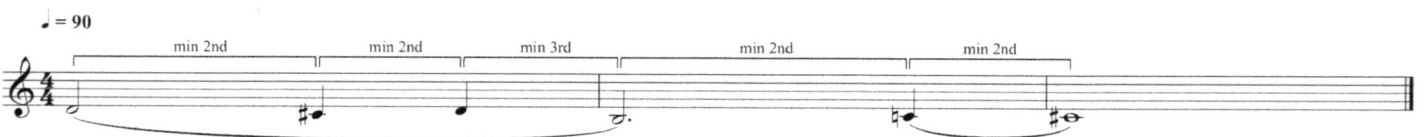

What might be more practical is an "inexact inversion", where you change the intervals from major to minor (or vice versa), to fit the key that you're in:

Example 5p:

An inexact inversion of Example 5p would make sure it kept to the notes of D Major:

Example 5q:

Creating An Ostinato From a Melody

Perceived change from original material: Slight

A melodic idea can be turned into an ostinato, making it available to use for accompaniment elsewhere in the score. Let's use the examples below as our melodic idea:

Example 5r:

To smooth out this ostinato you may decide to fill the rhythmic spaces by repeating notes...

Example 5s:

...or coming back to the root note:

Example 5t:

These are just two ideas of many, of course!

Rhythmic Transformation

Perceived change from original material: Slight to considerable

You can change things by shortening the rhythm of your theme, like this:

Example 5u:

Example 5v:

Personally, I've not used this approach much. A more useful approach is to extend the idea, which creates some harmonic shifts. This can be very helpful when you need to fill in with some music underneath dialogue, but retain the feel and atmosphere of the theme.

Have a look at Example 5w below, then compare it with the extended version I've created for Example 5x.

Example 5w:

Example 5x:

Time Signature Transformation

Perceived change from original material: Slight to considerable

You may also want to experiment with changing the time signature of your melody. You could experiment to see how it works with a 3/4 feel, or add some space with a 6/4 feel. Here is what Example 5w might sound like in 3/4 and 6/4:

Example 5y:

Example 5z:

Experiment and Be Musical

I hope that some of the ideas here have sparked your imagination. My aim isn't to turn you into a prescriptive composer who declares part-way through a score, "And now, I shall go retrograde!"

The aim is for you to experiment with and absorb these concepts to see which ones you like and find useful. Then make them your own, change them, use them to find creative and musical options with which to enhance the story of the show you're scoring.

Chapter Six – Intros and Outros, Builds and Reveals

Each cue you write will need to be designed to fit a specific start-point and end-point in a scene. In between these two points you will probably have to build up the music in some way, whether that's creating a climax to match a revelation on screen, or a drop-off to match a change of direction in the scene.

In this chapter we'll look at the challenges these moments can pose to a TV composer and some effective ways to approach them.

Spotting Sessions

Often in film and TV, the director and composer will get together for a *spotting session*. This is essentially a meeting where the two share their ideas about where music is going to occur in the show, where cues should start and finish, and what the music should do.

Now, of course, every show and genre are different, but in the world of documentaries I've scored (large and small), do you know how many spotting sessions I've had? None!

They are popular within the feature film process, and also episodic drama series, but for many TV shows, the consensus seems to be that there's no time to sit and talk about this stuff – we can work it out as we go. Instead, I often receive a rough cut of footage that has been edited with temp music on. Along with this comes a Word document via email with a list of timecodes, showing where the music cues should start and end.

Timecode

Whether you have the luxury of a spotting session or not, when you get footage through to score there should always be a little clock running somewhere on screen, often in the top corner (this gets removed from the show once it's ready for broadcast). The composer and the production team use this clock to refer to exact parts of the film by their timecode point.

Timecode is a string of numbers that look like this: 01:46:32:11. In this examples it means you are one hour, forty-six minutes, thirty-two seconds and eleven frames into the film.

When you're first working on early edits from your production team, you'll usually find that their descriptions of entry and exit points for the music only refer to the minutes and seconds part of the timecode (e.g. "music to start at 11:25"), or they'll give you a visual cue, for example, "The music should start once the glass hits the bar."

Effective Intros

"I am obsessed with how you get in and get out of things, I don't like hearing cues start and I don't like hearing them stop unless there's a good reason. That's difficult to do." – Michael Price

The way you begin a cue in a TV show is important and often isn't as easy as you'd think. A lot of the time, especially with drama cues, you're looking for ways to ease the music in, under-the-radar. I would estimate that for these kind of genres, creeping the cue in like this accounts for over eighty percent of music entry points.

So why is this "creeping in" method so popular?

When using music to enhance the emotion in a show, we usually don't want the viewer to even perceive that the music is there. The purpose of the music is to engage the viewer further in the action and we certainly don't want to distract them from their immersion in the show. The most likely cause of unwanted distraction will be the entry point of the cue.

Remember in Chapter Two we discussed the power of contrast – going from one thing to something totally different? Here is the point at which contrast can work *against* us, as we move from having no music to introducing the cue.

To that end, it's common to opt for the most simple, unobtrusive musical option in order to sneak in a cue. Movement is often out. Thick, complex or multi layered textures aren't ideal either.

A single sustained note with a soft timbre is one very common way. We're talking about a hollow sounding synth pad note, or perhaps a solitary string note. Even then, the introduction of music into a scene is meaningful, so you and the production team will often decide on which (or after which) event on screen, or line in the script, the music should enter.

An effective and little-discussed secret for these sneak-in cues is to wait for a second or so after the on-screen event that signals the cue, then introduce the music. While you will have sat through this scene a hundred times already in the studio, when it airs viewers will be seeing it for the first time, and this pause is incredibly effective. It takes the human brain a small chunk of time to process what has just happened and react emotionally. Having that small note hit them at the exact same time they process an emotion or reaction to what is on screen can be the perfect moment.

Another option to sneak in a cue is to find another sound to "hide under". For example, if you are trying to sneak in with a low-tension drone sound, and the scene has a car engine starting up, you can conceal the start of the music by fading it up from under the engine sound. Be aware of these sound FX opportunities, but you have to get a little lucky within a scene – they need to happen just as you want to start your music!

Michael Price offers this golden advice:

"I've got one top tip and once I tell you this everybody is going to be doing it forever!

It's just as a little techie thing: I use filters all the time. So pretty much every sound, if I'm generating stuff out of the computer, then I'll have a low pass filter on it – that's the one where I take the top off. So rather than just turning something down [to end a cue] so that I've got a bright sound getting quieter, I'll always filter them so that they actually get duller as well as get quieter. And I'll do the same thing on the way in as well.

Now, you can't do it too quickly, otherwise it sounds a bit 'swooshy' if you've got too much resonance on there. But a combination of using filters to try and make a tail that disappears, and often automating reverb as well, so that things get more reverberant [works well]. So that they kind of disappear backwards rather than just stop.

So in a way that's a sonic thing more than a musical thing, but if you open up one of my Logic sessions, everything is automated all the time and often the reverb and filters are automated as well."

Exceptions To The "Sneak In" Intro

"More times than not, the way into a cue is that the cue sort of sneaks and creeps in without announcing itself, and then there it is. But of course it just depends on what's needed. Sometimes the cue will just come right in to do its job." – Mac Quayle

As Mac Quayle points out, there are exceptions to the "sneak in" rule. Leaping in full force with music will probably be a shock to the system for the viewer. Maybe you want that. Some examples might be:

- Moments to intentionally shock, such as a climactic horror sequence intended to scare an audience

- Entertainment, sports, game shows or reality shows where you want to grab attention

- Commercials, where things need to get to the point straight away in a short period of time.

Alternatively, you may need to find the middle ground between a sneak-in and coming in full force. Walter Murphy says this is often the case in the animation shows he regularly scores.

"In a twenty-one minute animated network show, everything is contracted. No scene is longer than a minute to a minute-fifteen and shifts in tone happen rather quickly. So you don't have time: you have to get to the musical point a lot faster than you would otherwise.

With this type of animation [Family Guy and American Dad], it's a little less subtle than what you'd do on a dramatic show or on a documentary. It's pretty on the nose.

Usually there's a joke and then the music responds, or there are a few quasi-tender moments in American Dad or Family Guy and I just try to gently enter and exit, as if it were a realistic, dramatic, heartfelt movie."

Intros Case Study: Documentary Journeying Sequences

In the type of documentary I've worked on, it's not uncommon to have "transitioning" sequences crop up in each episode. For example, in one documentary I scored, the show would look at a specific topic or story for a while, then cut to some awe inspiring aerial footage moving swiftly over different landscapes. These sections visually transitioned us from one story to the next and the music needed to do the same.

The production team and I decided to come back to a "journeying" piece of music for these sequences. (As a side point, a journeying melody wasn't appropriate, as the transitioning sections were always narrated with facts about the landscape or what we were about to see next. Instead, a recurring, sound-bed track served the same purpose).

When considering the intro for this journeying track, it became clear that the piece shouldn't creep in as the footage began, because as soon as those awe inspiring shots happened we were visually "out of the door" and on our way. It was supposed to be immediately exciting.

However, the sequence of the show prior to these journeying transitions would be different each time. We might be coming out of a sequence where there had been music up until the end, or where there hadn't been music at all for several minutes. Perhaps the previous sequence was a fun story, or at other times, a tragic one.

Added to this, there was sometimes a "hard cut" in the edit of the film. In other words, it went straight from the scene before into the impressive aerial shots. In other places it was more gradual: the camera shot might, for example, rise off the ground before we took off into the big money vistas.

I'll break down for you my methods for approaching the intros for this journeying track.

First, I realized that, given the above variables, I needed a few options for the intro(s), so that I could select them on a case by case basis.

I copied some light percussion (drums played with brushes), out of the main section of my journeying piece and pasted it in for about two bars ahead of the main, fuller section of the track.

This served to put our journey into first gear and get us moving with some light movement, without the shock of dropping the full track in. So we were off and running, but also easing in the music. I had another version where this intro percussion was replaced by a rhythmic line on a pan flute. This gave me two options if I felt one didn't work as an intro for a particular sequence.

Here is an example of what a track might sound like with just the drums at the start:

Example 6a:

This was the version with the pan flute replacing the light percussion:

Example 6b:

There is a great advantage to using a looping rhythmic idea here. You don't need to have an exact one or two bars before the main body of the track subsequently enters. Yes, if it falls in between anything more than an eighth note beat, that won't feel as smooth a transition for the listener, but if it works better to picture, there's nothing stopping you using a few bars and a few beats worth of a light percussive intro to best fit the scene.

The above idea, coming in with the smaller movement of the pan flute or percussion, seemed to work best when starting those moments directly on an edit point – i.e. the visuals changed to the landscape shots and musically, the light movement started.

While it's a rookie error to be obsessed with having something musical happen on every cut in a sequence in TV scoring, hitting this cut into the aerials every time was logical here: you wouldn't want to feel you were obviously journeying before or after your eyes told you that you were!

So, onto the next challenge. What if the journeying sequence is coming out of a section with no music, or a particularly emotional moment where even the light percussion will feel like a "jolt" to the listener?

Here, you simply use a "sneak-in" technique from earlier in the chapter. The light percussion provides a way of easing into the full track, but given that we want the drums to coincide exactly with the aerial shots, it's often fine to start that sneak-in element – with, say a simple high synth pad note – under the final moments of the scene before as a little transitional glue.

Example 6c:

Lastly, there might be the odd moment where you need to come in more obviously on the journeying sequence. This would be appropriate when there has been full music in the sequence that precedes the journey, and so moving to light percussion would feel like a downwards gear shift.

In such cases, if there is a little silence between the last scene's music and the entry of the full journey theme, it's still nice to ease in the listener by adding a brief effect. This could be a reverse effect (for example reversed low, octave piano notes), for just a second or two, to reduce any jolt between scenes.

You've probably noticed that one of the main takeaways here is that "no music, then music" equals a jolt – the contrast effect, but not in a good way. Occasionally a jolt might be called for as an effect, but the vast majority of the time it is to be avoided and we don't want the audience to be aware that our music is there. This is at the core of the challenge of writing good intros to TV cues.

Effective Outros

"With a lot of the stuff that I write… at the end it rings out into the next scene or just sort of dissipates. But of course it just depends on what's needed.

I was working on Mr Robot with Sam Esmail, the creator of that show. In the first season I noticed he was particular about how cues ended. What felt normal to me [was] to have it just ring out and die out – but he hated it!

He'd say, 'The cue needs to have an ending! Somehow it needs to end!' And so we worked on that a lot in the first season and I think it was pretty painful for both of us! So he became fond of finding something happening in the scene to cut off the cue abruptly.

He would love to do things like [for instance] the character is writing in a notebook and they close the notebook, then right as they close the notebook the music comes off. It doesn't matter if it's in the middle of a phrase, it's off! Or a door shuts… music: cut!

That can be a fun way to get out of a cue and have it end that way rather than it fading out or coming to some sort of resolution." – Mac Quayle

As Mac points out, letting the tail notes of a track ring a little into the next scene is a common and natural way of ending a cue. I've experimented over the years with the last note of a track being played before the next scene starts (so the music is over when the next section of the show begins), on the change, or a little into the next scene (the latter seemingly most effective when nothing too immediate or important happens at the start of the next sequence). Every case is different and depends on both the show and the track, so a little experimentation is often the best way here.

As we've covered, starting a track with all guns blazing has a dramatic effect on the viewer and applying this to the end of a cue (a "hard out") can also be dramatic.

Imagine some aerial camera footage, such as in our journeying example. The track is going full throttle as the pictures travel over the land, then the camera dramatically takes us off a cliff edge and the shot now transitions over gentle ocean waters. Travelling off the cliff edge might be an appropriate moment to pull all the elements of the track out (aside from perhaps a solitary high note, should reducing the music to nothing be too stark). This would serve to emphasize the drama of that moment.

Standard, ring-out endings are generally easier to execute and more elegant if you've subtly thinned out the track beforehand, stripping out some elements before the end. Movement is a consideration here too. Just as a viewer can feel movement when it starts, they may also feel it when it ends, so if you choose to end the movement in your track as you're stripping out elements in preparation for the ending, be mindful of where you choose to do this. Think about the contrast it will create.

As you may be realizing, elements that have an impact when you introduce them, can have an equal impact when you remove them. The listener can hear the hole created by their absence. But the methods you used to introduce elements smoothly can hold the key to making your track end smoothly when applied in reverse. Every cue and every scene is different so, as always, be led by the show and the story.

Building Music in a Scene

Most of the time your music will need to build underneath a scene. It might be a small swell up and down to punctuate the emotion within a tender scene, or on the other end of the spectrum, it might build relentlessly to a dramatic ending.

The build might flow, introducing elements "under the radar", or you may wish to more obviously change gear at certain moments in the sequence. There are many ways to build a piece of music, of course, but let's take a closer look at the effect of layering elements in your tracks.

Modular Layering

Some scenes benefit from a modular approach to building the music. Put another way, this just means viewing your track in blocks. This can be most effective in movement-orientated tracks, as well as longer cues that require you to structure the build over a longer chunk of time.

Perhaps layer one is your pulse, layer two is some reversed piano, layer three an acoustic guitar and so on.

Example 6d

You may wish to sketch out your layers ahead of writing to picture, so that you can introduce different layers as you go, dragging elements in your DAW and trying out different blocks that enter and exit at different times.

If you find things are starting to sound a little predictable using this approach, experiment with writing some parts to repeat in different rhythmic groupings, such as 2 or 3 beats to each pattern, if other parts are in 4.

Example 6e:

The Sonic Spectrum: Keeping Out of Your Own Way

Whether using a modular layering approach, or another method of composition to build your music, be wary of adding too many instruments that occupy the same sonic range. It's really easy to end up with a track that sounds muddy. Below is a diagram showing the frequency range of some of the most popular instrument choices in TV Soundtrack work:

Example 6f: [see opposite page]

Musical Instrument Range Chart

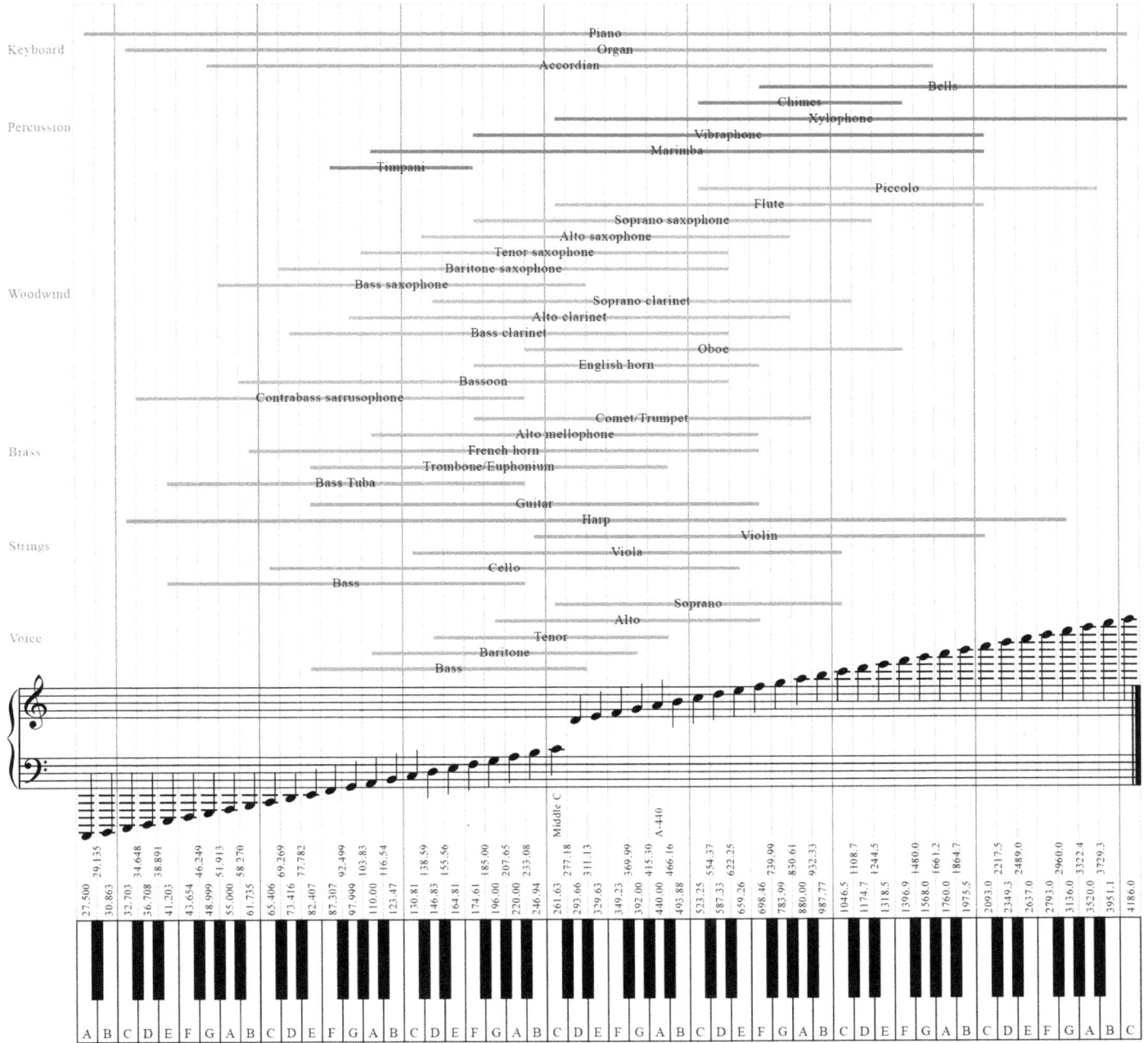

Clearly some instruments, such as the piano and guitar, have wide ranges to choose notes from, while others are much narrower. Consider these ranges when making decisions about what instrument layers to add.

If you're set on instrument choices with ranges that cross over, consider going to your EQ plugin and experiment with "carving out" i.e. reducing certain frequencies in one instrument to allow another instrument to breathe. I've found this to be more of an art than a science, so trust your ears and make sure you're not making things worse by removing the fundamental characteristics of the instruments!

If you're using a modular layering approach, the introduction of a new instrument or layer to build the track may best coincide with the removal of another layer at that point, especially if it occupies a competing range. Making room for a new instrument in this way can help keep a mix clean. Layering doesn't mean that in order to build a track, every new instrument that is introduced has to stay in – just be aware that removing more dominant instrument layers (such as drums) will be more obvious and therefore create a "change of gear" rather than a gradual transition.

Reveals And Transitions

Your music will often need a climactic section or moment, or perhaps several, depending on the show's content. Either way, it's good to have some options for achieving this. Remember that these moments (often used to "reveal" imagery, or to signify a pivotal fact revealed by the narrator, or both) don't always have to be huge musical moments. They could be, if the reveal needs to be accentuated, but smaller reveal moments can still add excitement. This is one of the big advantages to using bespoke music for a production rather than library music, which would be much harder to cut to a scene like this.

Choose Your Moments

There will be moments when the music can serve to add a little lift or transition to a certain section in a show, but be thoughtful and selective as to where you try to insert these. Adding too many moments into your score that sound like musical reveals when they're not needed will lessen the impact of necessary musical reveals. They can also make your track feel over-the-top, unsettled and generally too keen! Sometimes the music just needs to sit and wait, serving as a background to the other elements of the production.

If you are listening back to work you've created to picture, and you feel that the music contains too many reveal moments, search for such moments that occur near to each other and see if one can be smoothed over. Or perhaps one is simply unnecessary because sounds effects or dialogue are doing the heavy lifting for you. Always consider the possibility that the show doesn't need the addition of music to achieve its goal at certain points.

Each situation is different and experimentation is always a good idea. Below are a few ideas you may for you to experiment with, for moments when your music needs to give the feeling that something has been revealed.

Bridging The Reveal

You may choose to have elements that happen before the reveal/transition and then bridge into it. This glues things together nicely and avoids shocking the listener too much.

For example, if the moment was magical, then soft cymbal rolls and glissandos (mark tree, harp, glockenspiel, etc.) might be effective. An ascending woodwind run could also be effective.

Larger scale grand reveals may be preceded by timpani and orchestral bass drum rolls with cymbal rolls, and a crescendo of brass or strings. Orchestral risers can be used if things need to get big. (Orchestral sample packs often contain these elements, which are usually strings, brass and woodwinds ascending in a somewhat disorganized way, which can add a lot of anticipation before a climactic moment. They're mostly heard in film trailers. Use sparingly, if at all within TV!)

Risers on a smaller scale (or achieved electronically) can be effective leading into a section, as can subtle reversed effects or instruments. Sustained instrument notes faded up after their initial attack can prove an effective lead-up to a reveal/transitions too.

Conversely, a measure of silence in a score before a moment of revelation can be incredibly effective in underlining the moment ahead. This is perhaps the most stark example of how taking away elements can create as dramatic an effect as adding them.

The addition or subtraction of elements can give the feeling to the viewer that something has changed, or is about to change, so be sure to experiment with what works for your particular scene.

It's often best to avoid being too heavy handed: the more elements that you use together, the larger the reveal is often going to be. Bear in mind that the music is not the only element in play, so make sure it fits in the overall effect and doesn't dominate or clash with the other elements.

As these elements are just a guide to what's popular, there is a chance that some may sound clichéd in certain settings, so use them as a point of inspiration rather than a set of rules.

Reveals As Transitions

By definition, a revelation usually leads to a change of some sort and can also mark a shift in the music. You may need to make a change of musical direction (such as a mildly tense scene turning sentimental or emotional), or a larger shift (such as that same mildly tense scene transitioning into an action sequence).

Animation can contain some of the starkest, quickest shifts, whether this is a reveal or a transition at a less obvious point. Walter Murphy explains how he approaches making these moments work in as seamless a way as possible:

"Animation can contain radical shifts in tone that you wouldn't do in serious film or a love story or anything like that. I had this one cue today where the cast are marching towards a spaceship in the sky and Roger [American Dad character] has this speech that's inspirational. The producers wanted the music to be mysterious, then uplifting, then switch to something that was Close Encounters-like. The challenge for me is to try and do those things and still make it sound like a cohesive piece of music.

To do that, sometimes you can make the rhythmic activity hold for a little bit and then transition harmonically to introduce the next idea. Just so it doesn't sound like you've snipped the Pro Tools file and come in with the next one!

There's no real rule to doing that; it's just practice. One of my techniques is that I wait until the next morning and then I listen back and I think, 'I could that better' or 'I could smooth that out a little more.'"

Chapter Seven – Production Toolkit

"Production is so important. I feel like we're composers and so we're writing music, but the music is being recorded or created in our computers and so it has to be produced: it has to sound good. It has to be arranged in a way that is clear and makes sense.

And so we need to be music producers. We need to be able to produce, we need to be able to engineer if we don't have an engineer that does all the mixing for us, it's so important.

I can't stress enough how much this is a big part of it. Because you can write this great piece of music, but if it hasn't been presented in a way that sounds professional and clear, big or small, whatever it's supposed to be, then it's not doing its job.

And the tools that I use to do that? It's nothing super fancy. I love reverb. I use a lot of different reverb plugins. I love delay. I love filters, EQ and compressors. All of those things I will use to shape the sound."
—Mac Quayle

As Mac points out, these days you have to be a music composer *and* a producer. Some would argue that since production led scores are so prevalent today, it's almost more important to be a great producer than a great composer. Either way, production has become a skill you can't ignore. You client will likely be used to hearing demos and mock-ups of music that sound as good as the real thing, so the way that you produce your music – that is, how you create and decide on different sounds, combine those elements and make the finished product sound great – has to be up to par.

In this chapter we'll deal with some of the essential elements to be comfortable with in terms of producing music for TV, and I'll share some tips, tricks and techniques that work well for this medium.

Essential Skill: EQ

"Sometimes a particular sound might have a pretty wide frequency range. And say I like it and it feels right, but the low frequencies are clashing, they're muddying up what I already have.

I'll just use an EQ or a filter and roll off the low frequency and now I'm just getting the mid range and highs of this sound and I've carved out room for it so it fits in there, and doesn't get in the way of the other parts." –Mac Quayle

EQ (equalization) is simply a tool to boost or cut certain frequencies in your sound, from low tones to high tones. You'll probably open up your EQ plug-in for one of two reasons:

- To boost or cut certain tones to allow that instrument to sit better in the mix. (For example, removing some of the low frequencies if they are clashing with other instruments in the mix or voiceover)

- To color the sound of an instrument artistically. (That is, to make it sound different than normal because you feel that would add interest or a certain flavor that you're going for)

I like to use an EQ with an analyzer, so I can clearly see the frequency ranges I'm moving in front of me:

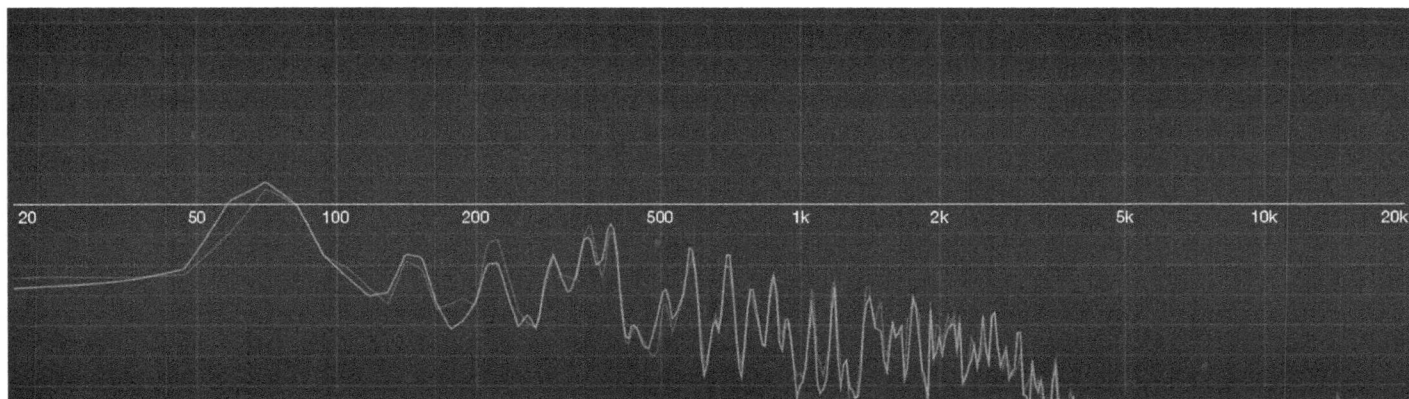

Low Pass and High Pass filters are useful when getting a mix right for a piece:

- A Low Pass filter cuts the high frequencies, allowing only the lower frequencies to pass through

- A High Pass filter works the opposite way, allowing only the higher frequencies through

You can control the frequency range of the highs or lows that are allowed to pass through the filter. Alternatively, you might decide to use your EQ plugin to attenuate some of the highs or lows.

More often than not, you'll be rolling off the low end (or using a high pass filter), as low frequencies can clutter a mix. You might want to keep dedicated low end aspects (like a kick drum), but even some bass tones can benefit from low end roll off. Often you won't even hear a big difference to begin with (and may be surprised how much low end can be rolled off before the sound loses warmth), but this will be effective in preventing the low end of the mix becoming muddy.

Using this method to "clean up" the low end of guitars and other instruments can give your mix a lot more overall punch. High pass filtering can also be useful to apply to your music to accommodate a low male voice narrating the show. You don't want to be competing with that!

Another technique for a clean low end mix is to slot various bass heavy instruments into different frequency regions using pitch and EQ controls, so they are not fighting each other for space in the low frequency range. In addition, it's often wise to avoid delay or long reverbs on low end instruments, as this can add to a cluttered, muddy low end.

When recording instruments, try to capture the best recording you can, rather than relying on EQ later to fix problems. If instruments are recorded well, little EQ should be needed. If you do apply EQ, then it's important to keep instruments sounding real and natural. Try not to boost/cut more than is absolutely necessary. One tip here is to boost/cut a wide rather than narrow spectrum. This will help keep the instrument's character intact.

One final tip: don't work on shaping your EQ whilst soloing the instrument in question (i.e. with other instruments muted). You might get things sounding great in isolation, but it still might not sit well in the mix. It's all about context. I've achieved some great sounding mixes where, if you solo the instruments, they sound thin and wiry. They sound great together in the mix, however, and that's all that matters.

Thickening The Low End

It may seem strange after the above warnings to now think about thickening the low end! But as with so many of the techniques in this book, it's all about context. While you never want to have a cluttered low end to a mix, if you have a simple low range instrument playing (especially in orchestral writing), a common technique is to thicken this part with a bass guitar or low bass synth, usually playing long, held notes. You're often looking for something subtle that shores up the low end and adds weight to proceedings.

"One of the things I've found, which is an orchestration and a mix note as well, is that getting a meaningful bottom octave is incredibly challenging when you're working in music that is going to be used in TV.

I've got a lot of vintage keyboards and some outboard gear. I find there's something about how broken some of my old keyboards are that generates more complexity with a single bass note, than a rather more pristine soft synth. Somehow then, when you start to roll the bottom octaves off, and if you effectively play [the mix] on a laptop, then an old synth bass note or something that's gone through some valves, or some distortion, or with extra harmonics on, will always stay better than a relatively clean soft synth.

You don't need to have all the vintage stuff. You can do it in the box. But you've got to be listening carefully to make sure that you're not just enjoying your studio if you've got speakers that will play low.

I've got a set of little Avantone monitors, small square near-field monitors. I tend not to listen to them all the time, but when I bounce down cues to play to the producers, I usually balance [the mix] on those small speakers. Because I'm thinking, 'What's it going to sound like when someone listens to this on a laptop on a train?' Which is inevitably what's going to happen!

It's the same thing with the orchestra: make sure that your voicings and your doublings don't rely too much on the extremes of registers to function. They need to function when those disappear." – Michael Price

As Michael points out, the are very practical reasons for taking care with the low end of a mix.

My first job was as an assistant to the late, great Michael Kamen. The assumption with Michael's amazing film scores was that people were going to watch them in the cinema – that you could put a 50Hz rumble in there and it would be amazing because everybody would be listening to it on huge speakers on the big screen.

If you put a 50Hz tone in a TV score, good luck with it, because nobody is hearing that!

Compression: A Case of Less is More

Compression is a tool that squashes a waveform. You can put it on individual instruments, or on groups of instruments, or even on your master bus (the channel that your entire mix is coming out of).

Many people think it makes a track louder, but it's actually making the peaks of your track quieter. This evens out a musical performance (whether played live or recorded on your computer) as if it were an automated volume fader. By squashing the waveform and evening things out in this way, you can then turn up the overall "even" performance.

As compression is often misunderstood, here's a quick guide to the five most important settings to understand.

- **Threshold.** Threshold controls how much compression is applied i.e. at what point it kicks in. Having the threshold at zero means you're getting no compression. By turning the threshold down a little you'll have soft compression (also known as light compression). This will squash down only the loudest peaks. Turn the dial down further and it will affect the next loudest peaks too. This will continue until you turn it to the point where you have no dynamics left.

- **Ratio.** Ratio is expressed in decibels. A ratio of 2:1 means that any signal exceeding the set threshold by 2db will be reduced down to 1db above the threshold. Or a signal exceeding the threshold by 6db will be reduced to 3db above it etc. So, 1:1 means no compression at all and the higher you go, (3:1, 4:1, 5:1 etc.), the stronger the compression. Use ratio in combination with the threshold: the threshold governs when the compressor kicks in (in terms of volume peaks) and the ratio governs how much you want to turn down the signal once it kicks in.

- **Attack and Release.** The faster the attack is set, the faster the compression will be applied to the audio. Think of it as how fast the compressor "grabs" the audio to squish it! The faster the release, the faster it lets go of the audio. A great way to study these settings is to use some of the presets on your compressor and see how they sound and what the settings are.

- **Gain.** Gain (alternatively called Makeup Gain on some compressors) allows you to turn the gain back up. I say "back up" since applying compression is actually making the peaks of your track quieter. This control enables you to revert the overall volume to where it was before you started compressing.

Compression can be good for making elements punch through a mix by levelling out the dynamics. If you are scoring an action scene or something else kinetic or rhythmically based, this can be great. It can also be useful to even out a performance a little in terms of loud and quiet sections.

But be careful!

Although any tool that makes mixing easier may seem like it should be a go-to every time, compression can also totally kill the vibe of a track. Since compression removes the peaks and troughs of a performance, it might squash the feel that created the emotion in your piece – and TV soundtrack work is often about generating emotion. You don't want compression to crush all the dynamics out of a performance!

Don't put compression on a track if you are unsure what it's doing or what you're trying to achieve by having it there. If you do apply compression, know that a little can go a long way.

Once you send a cue back to the production team, the editor will sit it in the show and the production team will decide if it works. Your music will eventually end up at the "dub" (part of the post-production process where dialogue, effects and music are combined and mixed). Sometimes you'll be asked to provide stems for this (audio files for each individual instrument or a sub-group of instruments – just the strings or just the synths etc.) – while other shows may just request a stereo mix.

Either way, you final mix needs to give the *dubbing mixer* (known as the *re-recording mixer* in the US) somewhere to go when mixing. A highly compressed mix with no dynamics may be great for a pop song, but isn't a good idea for soundtrack work.

If you've listened to film/TV soundtracks on their own, you may well be familiar with having to turn the volume up on your headphones for the first part of a track and down in the middle. Don't worry if the editing team have to do the same with your tracks.

Reverb

I often hear tracks from upcoming soundtrack composers that have too little or too much reverb applied. I'd love to give you the "perfect settings" that always work, but that's impossible. There are too many variables. Added to which, too much or too little reverb may be an artistic choice that sounds amazing in a particular context.

In general, however, using too little reverb on your samples may lead to them sounding too dry and therefore unrealistic. Using too much is going to wash out the sound, lose definition and cause mix issues.

If you're using samples to emulate real instruments (as the vast majority of us are doing), you're going to need a little reverb 99% of the time. Many composers and producers like to route the signals of these instruments to the same bus in their DAW and put the reverb onto that. It helps to keep a unified sound and makes sense – as though those instruments were recorded in a room together. In a live recording, you would hear the same reverb from that room on each instrument. That's not to say that you can't put more reverb on some instruments and less on others, or use different reverbs within a track. What sounds good is king. A lot of the time it's about using just enough reverb to sweeten the sound a little while retaining definition.

Panning

Panning (or moving elements in your track to the left or right) can be a helpful tool to add space and clarity to a mix. Here are a few tips to get the best results:

- First, don't assume everything needs to be panned and don't start with anything panned by default
- Keep low frequency elements such as the bass and kick drum centered. This keeps your mix tight and grounded. If your bass is coming from a stereo source such as a synth, consider converting or bouncing it to mono

- For the higher frequency instruments, it's often effective to separate those in the same frequency range (guitar and piano parts, for example). This will help them cut through

- Always reference your mix in mono as you go, to make sure you aren't making things worse with your panning decisions

- When writing a track with rhythmic elements, think about balance. Rhythmic elements that appear to be prominently on one side of a mix can be distracting. If you have, for example, hi-hats plus a shaker, separate them out a little, evenly to each side.

- Panning several stereo instruments, such as synths, can lead to the center of the mix getting cluttered and muddy.

Lastly, beware of hard panning anything totally to the left or right. I would go so far as to say, just don't do it – especially for film/TV where your music is part of a bigger picture and not meant to steal attention. Here's an interesting additional reason: in some situations, such as people sharing a set of earbuds, these instruments risk not being heard at all by one of the listeners!

Quantizing

Quantizing is another tool for which there is a time and a place. It can make or break your track depending on when and how you use it.

I am you are familiar with the quantize feature on your DAW: the ability to have the computer automatically move notes you've played to make them dead in time to a predefined note value such as a 1/16th note or 1/8th note, etc. Many composers go to the quantize button either too much, not enough, or at the wrong time.

In broad terms, if a track is supposed to primarily convey a tender, moving or sensitive feel (or some similar purpose) avoid quantizing. Like overdone compression, nothing will suck the emotion out of an emotional piano performance, for instance, that hearing it quantized like it was played by a robot. When humans perform music, it's not rhythmically perfect and the notes of a chord don't land together perfectly. Those elements are a large part of what gives a performance it's emotion.

If, however, a track is quite percussive or rhythmic by nature, quantizing is useful to keep things sounding clean and tight. In such instances, you may decide to keep most elements quantized and the odd element in upper registers (that catch the ear) un-quantized. This can neatly tread the line between a tight, focused overall sound, that doesn't sacrifice realism. You don't have to have either quantized or everything un-quantized.

Another thing to keep in mind is the amount of quantization. Many composers and producers forget that most DAW's have a quantize amount setting:

Experiment with this. You may, for example, quantize the drums and percussion in a track, but set rhythmic ensemble string lines to have a quantize strength of 80%. This might create enough tightness within the overall string performance, while allowing it to sound natural, as all the notes don't fall exactly together.

Adding Air To Samples

Sometimes you might want to take a part of your track, played with samples, and make it sound more like it was a live recording.

A neat trick is to solo the track, then record it coming out of the speakers in your room. You then put that track into your piece (with the original muted, of course!). This will add your room sound to the samples. It can help them to sound "live" and is a useful trick for making elements sound bigger in a production. It adds "air" to the sound and realism, and is often worth taking the time to do. I'd advise losing any reverb on the instrument before re-recording it, then you can decide later whether to add it back in.

Try this when you're not in the middle of a project, so you can get a better handle on when you might need to do it and when "in the box" will do just fine.

Opting For The Softer Samples

I know a number of composers (including a few Hollywood A-listers), who love the following technique. It yields some interesting results and flows nicely from the point above about trying to keep the realism in a track when using samples.

With most sample packs, you'll find the instruments have been multi-sampled at different velocities. An orchestral bass drum boom will trigger a different sample when you play it quietly, than if you hit the key with all your might. It's easier to hear the interesting overtones and nuances of an instrument generated from a quieter performance. The beauty of technology is that we can use the quieter samples and then turn up the volume in our mix. This adds a different dimension to the sound than just using the louder samples.

Of course, be careful not to end up with a track that is unrealistic because you've combined a jumbled mess of soft and loud instrumental performances that are now all at the same level! Also, there are many times when this technique is not appropriate, and you want those loud sampled sounds. But, using samples of a softer dynamic range can add intimacy and color to your music. As always, let the context of the show be your guide.

Overlapping Long Midi Notes (Orchestral Samples)

When dealing with orchestral samples, I'm a big fan of overlapping midi notes in many situations. The next chapter will deal in greater length with the subject of orchestration, but let's look at this briefly here in the context of production techniques.

Within orchestral samples, when MIDI looks like this…

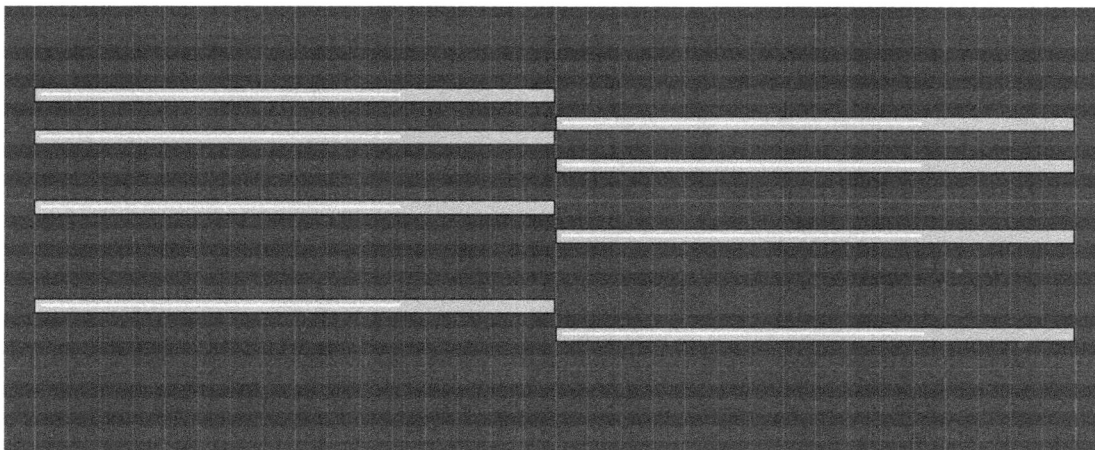

…I can tell it's not going to sound as realistic as it could.

The orchestral samples available today are pretty amazing, mainly as you're simply triggering a real recording of some strings, brass or whatever it is that you choose. With everything but shorter samples, you'll notice that the notes often creep in ever so slightly after you trigger them. That's great, as it mimics what real players would do when they *start* playing. The issue is that when the sampling recordings are made, performances by the players are started from silence, as opposed to coming onto that note from a previous note.

One thing that I hear a lot that gives away a track as being obviously created with orchestral samples is when chords change. If you play in your MIDI as per the above image, there will be a small, uniform space as the strings release together and then come in exactly together. The delayed start of the samples will leave a gap.

To avoid this and allow a smooth transition between chords, I nearly always go back over what I've just played in, set my DAW's MIDI drag settings out of "snap to grid" mode (so I can move the start and end of notes freehand), then drag the beginning of notes forward a little and end of notes back. Let your ears be your guide. The end result – something that changes chord seamlessly to the ear – will often end up looking a bit like this:

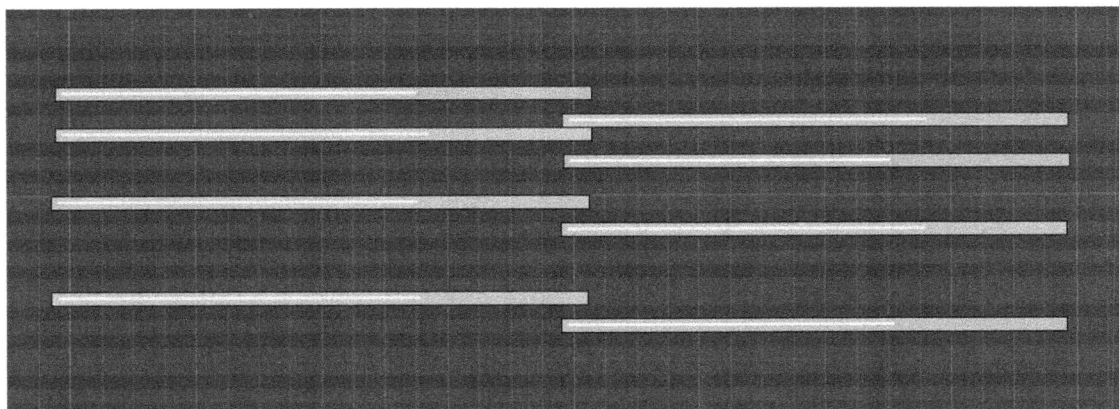

Reference Track Comparison

One of the best pieces of advice I can give you when mixing your music is to have another track similar to the kind of sound you're trying to achieve (perhaps the temp track if you're staying close to that), loaded into your DAW for reference. Once you're done writing your track and you're in the mixing phase, refer to this track regularly, *playing it on the same monitors as your track and at the same volume.*

Use your ears to gauge the difference in level between instruments, study EQ choices, and identify any other mix or production factors. Run an EQ with a visual analyzer on both your track and the reference track, and look at which frequencies differ. There are a variety of tools and plugins on the market that can help make such referencing easier.

Mastering

People often ask how to, or if they should master a track for TV.

You'll remember from our discussion on compression that we don't want to rob a track of all its dynamics and therefore emotion. We're not making a pop record. That said, myself and a good few other TV composers I know, do like to add a little bit of "magic" to at track at the final stage. We're all different, so I'll share what works for me.

First of all, what I do at this final stage varies wildly depending on what kind of track it is. For soft, simple, emotional stuff, or orchestral music, I'm hardly going to do anything. What I will do (and this applies to pretty much all soundtracks I'm producing), is add just a little high end boost to the whole track. Hardly any, maybe just +0.5db to +1.0 db to the top end of things on the master channel. My reason for this is that I don't like it when tracks sound muffled and I don't know if the monitors in the edit suites (or any system used by a client for evaluating my music), are a little duller than mine. In addition, when comparing home studio tracks to temp tracks, many home studio tracks sound a little duller, so I try to compensate for that just a little.

I might then add a limiter onto the master bus. This is more of a safety measure to prevent the peaks of a track going over the threshold, and is not always necessary.

For tracks that are more contemporary (Rock, Pop, EDM, etc.), I might add a little light compression on the final mix, just to glue everything together. Personally, I'm not against bringing up a mastering chain preset and seeing how it sounds, then tweaking from there. (Most DAWs and effects plugins have preset chains programmed that you can drop onto a track, which usually contain EQ, a compressor and a limiter. Or you could look into the excellent third party mastering products by companies such as Waves and Ozone). If there was a temp track on the sequence originally, I always A/B against that and try to get the sound in that ballpark. Again, be sparing with compression!

Personally, I think it's important to see this final stage more as fine-tuning the overall sound than making sweeping changes.

"At the final processing stage I will do what I call mix bus processing. Which is a way of coloring the sound just to give it a little more finished frequency content. Almost like if you were recording music for release as a CD or an album, then the final process there is mastering: people go and they tweak the frequencies and compress and limit or whatever. So I will do something like that as the last stage and it just helps it sound more finished, more polished. All that stuff is important to keeping the people I'm working for happy." – Mac Quayle

Chapter Eight – Orchestration Toolkit

Many TV soundtracks call for the composer to mix orchestral elements with more modern sounds, such as loops and synths. TV composers who are required to do this kind of hybrid writing tend to have some great orchestral samples at their disposal, but even the best samples can make for a poor track if they are not used in an authentic way.

I have personally heard tracks that don't sound good written by people who were using expensive, cutting edge samples and, equally, great tracks by people using cheaper sample sets. My advice is to buy the best orchestral samples you can afford, but whatever you do, learn as much as you can about how to make them sound great. This chapter will cover some of the techniques and orchestration knowhow required to make your orchestral samples sound great and can, of course, be transferred to using live players too, if you have that option open to you.

Keep in mind that orchestration is a huge topic. (The fact that people have full-time jobs as orchestrators should tell you this). As such, this chapter is a "toolkit" rather than an in-depth study of the art. Its aim is to provide you with practical tips, tools and advice to help you use orchestral elements in your soundtrack work.

Strings

The most commonly called for orchestral element in a hybrid or straight classical soundtrack is usually strings. They are booked for more TV/film sessions than woodwind or brass, so I'll spend some time covering how to create great sounding string parts for your piece.

First, let's get familiar with the main string techniques. Your sample library may well categorize its sounds using these playing methods. Understanding what these techniques are and what sound they can deliver means you can approach your sound selection from a more interesting and creative point of view.

String Techniques

Arco

This simply means the standard string playing technique using the bow.

Pizzicato

Most people are familiar with this sound, created by the player plucking the strings with their fingers. This light sound is often used within "dramedy", comedy, and other delicate applications, but is popular so can turn up just about anywhere else.

This technique is lighter and therefore quieter than playing full-on with the bow. Many composers, even when recording live strings, tend to beef up pizzicato lines with samples later, or sometimes replace the live ones completely. One reason for this is that it can be difficult for a large section to play such short notes exactly together, so if that's the effect you need, samples can be a good way forward, plus they offer a more upfront "in your face" sound for dramedy and comedy.

To keep pizzicato writing realistic, be careful not to write passages that are fast, as these can quickly become impossible for players because of the technique involved.

Con Sordino

In Italian, "con sordino" means "with the mute". This mute is a small device that the player attaches near the bridge of the instrument. Sordino strings have an almost veiled sound, different from when the players perform without the mute.

This technique can work beautifully for more intimate sounding tracks, though it doesn't necessarily mean the players have to play quietly.

Tremolo

Tremolo is the shimmering tone caused by moving the bow backwards and forwards quickly. It's often used during suspense or tension moments in film/TV soundtracks.

Vibrato

Much like an opera singer may use vibrato with their voice, a string player can wobble their finger on the fingerboard of the instrument in varying amounts to achieve a similar effect. This produces an expressive sound and can be particularly useful on solo string lines to add emotion and realism.

A player will often start a note then add vibrato once it's held, so you should approach this in the same way.

Portamento

Portamento is when the player glides up or down the fingerboard from one note to the next. You might choose to milk this effect if you wanted a gypsy style fiddle performance, or add it into a solo string line here and there to taste. It's nice to add a little realism to things, but needs to work in context as an effect. You can often set up your string plugin to use portamento between overlapping notes should you wish.

Legato

Smooth playing between notes, often minimizing the amount of bowing used for many notes.

Staccato

The opposite of legato, with each note detached or separated from the others. It has a spikey sound.

Spiccato

Spiccato is a bowing technique where the bow appears to bounce lightly on the string. It's a commonplace technique used to create rhythmic string ostinatos. It's worth trying out your spiccato patch first if that's that sound you are going for.

Col Legno

This is where the performer plays the strings with the wood of the bow as opposed to the hair of the bow. This creates a faint, whispery, white noise effect, often used in horror and sci-fi scenes.

Sul Tasto

This is where the bow is played over the fingerboard and produces a soft, thin tone. "Flautando" is also an instruction to bow over the fingerboard to create a flute-like tone. These techniques can be effective and atmospheric.

Sul Ponticello

Often shortened to "Sul Pont", this is the technique of keeping the bow near the bridge to bring out the higher harmonics and produces a slightly nasal tone.

Harmonics

An eerie, hollow, glassy sound made by bowing while the left hand is touching lightly on the string.

Remember that it's perfectly acceptable to combine several of these techniques. You might have some pizzicato going on in the low strings, tremolo in the violas, with the violins holding a high note flautando.

Using String Samples Effectively: Small Ensembles

The above definitions will allow you to seek out different sounds in your samples, but there are a few things to keep in mind to achieve a truly realistic string sound.

First of all, you will find that large ensemble strings are easier to make sound authentic than smaller ensembles. Many top sample libraries are aware of this and have released products dedicated to smaller ensemble groups. While large ensemble can be the go-to for film scores (perhaps a symphony orchestra grouping of 16 first violins, 14 second violins, 12 violas, 12 cellos and 10 double basses), the more intimate sound of a smaller ensemble can be effective for TV (perhaps 2 first violins, 2 second violins, 2 violas, 2 cellos and 1 double bass).

The best way of bringing string samples to life (especially for smaller ensemble writing) is to get at least one real string player in there. The difference can be astonishing! With careful mixing, the real string player(s) can be sunk into the mix to the point where it doesn't sound like that instrument is a solo line, but the intricacies and imperfections of its performance still catch the listener's ear, adding realism, and with the samples adding the ensemble "bulk".

When doing this, a composer friend of mine likes to opt for viola as his real instrument. His reasoning is that the ear is drawn to higher register instruments, but a violin is often the highest, so risks being heard as a solo line if it's replaced with a live player. Going one instrument lower (viola), allows for an easier blend.

Using String Samples Effectively: Large Ensembles

When adding a real player to bring a smaller, sample string ensemble to life, what we're doing is adding the complexity and imperfections that the human ear associates with live performance.

We want to carry this philosophy over to larger string sections too. One way to do this is to avoid the impulse to use the ensemble patch that your sample library gives you, but to record the violin lines with the ensemble violins patch, then the violas with the ensemble violas patch and so on. This creates realism, as those different samples will move at slightly different times and at slightly different volumes – which is what a real section would do.

Another effective way to achieve these imperfections is to blend together the strings from more than one string library. You might choose to play violin string samples from library A, but violas from library B, cellos from library A, and then basses from library B. Routing them all to the same reverb after doing this will help restore the balance of a unified sound.

Articulations Are A Must

Watch footage of any TV/film composer at work with their orchestral samples and you'll see their left hand on their mod wheel or a fader. They are moving around an articulation for that sound.

If you're not using articulations (a lot!), then your orchestral samples (not just your strings) are not going to sound anywhere near as realistic as they could. Articulations are often assigned to your mod wheel or other midi controllers and allow you to adjust dynamics, tremolo, articulation changes and a whole host of other elements in an organic sounding way. Oftentimes you may go back and record a second automation on that track (such as adding vibrato on a solo violin line while you're playing it in, then going back in to add articulations for dynamics).

In any recording, a musician's performance moves and breathes. Held string notes have points where players come to the end of their bows; brass and wind players have points where they need to breathe. While elements like these are less noticeable in a section than a solo performance (as multiple players will breathe at different times etc.), MIDI generated samples that don't sound like they are moving in volume and articulation can sound fake.

I'm not suggesting that you need to get into such detail that you try to make a sample sound like the bowing is beginning and ending, but moving articulations (usually dynamic changes) as you're playing your samples in is something you should be doing regularly.

Real Strings

If you have the budget to record more than just one or two string players to blend into your string samples, the following tips may be of use when writing for strings ahead of the recordings. They also help achieve realistic sounding mock-ups even if you don't have the budget for actual players. (I'd definitely recommend getting the advice of, or employing an orchestrator to help you between finishing your writing for live strings and printing parts for your session).

Divisi

When writing for strings you essentially have five "voices": first violins, second violins, violas, cellos and basses. If you have a chord with one or more of these sections playing two notes or more in a real life situation, you'd need to divide that section up. For example, get half the violas to play one note and half to play the other.

Diving a section up like this is called playing "divisi". A section playing divisi will naturally sound quieter and thinner, as there are less players per note. The beauty of samples is that you're not constricted by such a scenario. Then again, if realism is your aim, you may want to keep this factor in mind.

Agility and Switching Techniques

First violins and cellos are most used to playing virtuosic passages in music, so you may want to place most of that type of writing with them. If you are writing fast runs, sticking to scales makes this easiest for the players.

If you are asking a player to switch to/from mutes (sordino) or from a technique that requires the bow to one that doesn't (arco to pizzicato, or vice versa), allow half a bar to a bar form them to make that change.

Briefing The Players

"I've done a lot of hybrid scores – mixing real players with samples. Getting that to work has been interesting over the years.

What I've found with [combining] live strings with sampled strings is that a lot of the skill in doing that effectively is about what you tell the players, how you conduct and how you run the session.

The smaller the group of players, the more the players naturally play out in quite a soloistic way. So if you've got less than thirty strings, they feel like they want to fill the room: it's a natural thing to do and they're not doing anything wrong, they're giving everything they've got for you. But as you start to get down to twenty [players], twelve, eight, seven or even just a quartet, then if you're wanting to blend those with samples later on, you're asking the players to not play as if they're soloists. You're asking them not to play to fill the room.

You're more saying to them: 'How would this feel if you were sitting four back [in an orchestral section] and there were fifty of you? How would you be thinking about blending your sound? What would the bow speed be like? How much vibrato would you be using? How much would you project?'

And so a lot of time we've spent on string sessions that we are going to blend with some samples later on has been trying to get something sonically smooth and doesn't project too much and doesn't cut through too much, so then you can use that as a layer that enhances your samples. " – Michael Price

Mixing and Blending Samples With Live Players

"The mix I do on an absolute cue by cue basis. There will be cues that emotionally work perfectly with a dozen string players just on their own – you want to hear those individual voices. And there will be cues where you need a little help from our sampled friends underneath, just for a bit more weight and substance and to throw it into the background a bit more.

There's no right or wrong to that at all. It's just about letting your ear and your emotions guide you.

In a way, MIDI orchestration becomes mixing all in the same breath. We're all mixing as we're going effectively, even if you do hand off to a mixer to do the final [mix]. The speed everybody is going, you're making all of those sonic and orchestration decisions and they are much one and the same thing now.

I don't know many TV composers who are working in the way that film composers might have worked twenty years ago when they do a basic piano or string pad demo and then an orchestrator or themselves would flesh it out for seventy-five people with lots of new colors.

I think we're all doing photo-realistic demos right now for sign-off and then we're playing as much as we can, if time and budget allows, on top of it.

I think of the majority of composers working in TV scoring now, we're trying to create a final mix of whatever synth elements we've got, whatever samples we've got and whatever real instruments we've got that will translate the emotional message that we need when played through a probably not optimum playback system!" –Michael Price

Using Samples To Supplement The Live Orchestra

If you have the luxury of an orchestra and a score that isn't hybrid in nature, you may decide to use samples as more of a practical consideration:

"I'm usually supplementing the orchestra. For example, today I didn't have a harpist: American Dad has a somewhat smaller orchestra. So maybe I add an extra horn or something, so I brought [as samples] all the harp music and the celesta music. So that's the luxury of having samples at home so you can supplement it.

And then each show that I do has a fair amount of Pop music or some kind of electronic music which I do at home. I don't take up any orchestra time, any 'stage time' to do that.

After doing this for years and years I can pretty much determine how much music I can record in three hours because I only have three hours with the orchestra. It's one three-hour session per episode and usually Family Guy takes all three hours because there are generally between twenty and thirty-five pieces of music in every twenty-one minute show. Some of them are only five or eight seconds long, but since many of them are so different from each other it takes a long time to set them up.

We're lucky to have a group of great musicians every week that just play anything." – Walter Murphy

Brass

As mentioned, this chapter is more of a toolkit than a thorough exploration of orchestration. So here are some tips to get you started when using brass in your tracks. Remember that the use of brass within certain contexts can create heroic, regal or other associations that you may or may not want in your track, so keep any such potential associations in mind!

One of the most common ways of integrating brass into your soundtracks is via long notes, where they operate as harmonic glue.

Horns

Horns have a full, round, rich sound. They are also some of the best blending instruments in the orchestra. Be careful not to write parts too high in their register, where the notes will start to sound thin, or too low, where they begin to sound hollow. It's also worth noting that it's hard for horns to play high register notes softly, or low register notes loudly.

You'll often have four horns in an orchestra so, within the right register, you can write a great sounding three or four tone chord. However, as with all the instruments in this chapter, just because you have four horns, doesn't mean you always have to write for all four horns!

Horns are sometimes considered the midway point between woodwinds and brass, and are also rich and lush solo instrument options.

Trombones

Trombone chords work well at any dynamic level and they sound amazing played quietly! You'll usually have two tenor and one bass trombone, making three note chords an option.

Like the horns, be careful of keeping them within an effective range (approximately C3 to E4). Closed voicings (see the section later in this chapter about chord voicings), work well in the lower to mid ranges of trombones.

Trombones blend well within the orchestra, that is until played loudly, where their tone can get brassy, leading them to stick and blend less well (which could be great if that's what you are going for!)

Trumpets

Trumpets can be great for solo and melodic lines, but work less well as "harmonic glue" as their bright tone tends to stand out, rather than blend. The lower range of a trumpet can lead itself nicely to noble and somber applications.

Blending Brass

You may find a useful brass patch amongst your samples that combines several instruments from the brass family, making your writing and orchestration a little easier. The only issue I've found with this is that sometimes (often halfway through a chord sequence), you'll actually hear the sound change, as some instruments go out of range and are taken over by others. This can be frustrating and pull focus from the smoothness of chord changes.

If you're blending different elements of the brass family, try to keep each within the sweet spots of their ranges, where they sound the fullest. Some people like to write keeping each group apart i.e. trombones lowest, then horns, then maybe trumpets. Some of these ranges (and therefore notes) may overlap, which is fine.

Other times, you may choose to blend the groups a little more, having them play the same notes on top of each other ("doubling"). You might, in that case, just keep to the three or four tones in your chord.

Woodwinds

Woodwinds differ in tonal color from each other quite a lot. (The way each instrument is played is an indication of how inherently different they are: one comprises a single reed, two of them rely on the vibration of two reeds, and the last is played like blowing air over the top of a bottle!) For this reason, they often don't quite blend as well as strings or brass do within the orchestra.

Members of the woodwind family can make excellent and lyrical choices for soloing instruments and are also characteristic for their short, staccato ensemble sound, amongst a variety of other uses.

Flutes

Most of us are familiar with hearing flutes in their middle register, where they have a high, rich tone and sit well within the orchestral balance. Playing in its low register, the flute struggles to compete on volume, but the tone is still lovely and rich. At the upper ends of its range the flute can be pretty shrill. However, when the orchestra is playing loudly, high flutes can double with other high lines to add some weight and cut to those upper register elements.

A piccolo goes above a flute's range by an octave and can again, brighten the upper parts of your track. Both the flute and the piccolo are instruments of considerable dexterity and can be used as "ear candy", playing fast trills and runs to add excitement to a track.

Oboes

The first of our double reed instruments. Opposite to the flute, the oboe is weak in its higher registers and strongest in its lower register. Some do associate these lower registers with a duck call type honk, however! Go an octave up from this honking low end and you'll find a sweet spot where the Oboe sounds lyrical and ethereal, especially when playing melodies over a quiet orchestral backing.

The oboe's slightly bigger brother the Cor Anglais (or English Horn if you're in the United States), doesn't suffer so much from the honking effect in its low end.

Clarinets

The single reed option of the woodwind family has a mysterious, deep and dark quality in its low register, albeit a little lower in volume than when played higher. In its middle register it can be soft, beautiful and lyrical, ascending to an almost soft trumpet-like quality as it gets a little higher than this, making it a lovely solo instrument option. Venture to the higher ends of its capability and it can get shrill, though played up here in a softer way it can give a flute-like sound.

Bassoons

Like the oboe, bassoons are double reed instruments. Also similar to the oboe, the bassoon is weak in its higher registers and strongest (and loudest) in its lower register. Many use the bassoon as the bass instrument of the woodwind, though it can play melodically too. Lower end staccato notes can sound similar to lower string pizzicato notes.

Doubling Woodwinds

Doubling woodwind instruments can be an interesting technique to use in your track. When one woodwind instrument plays in unison with another, the color of each is slightly blurred into a new sound. There is also nothing to stop you doubling parts an octave apart if the ranges of your woodwind choices causes issues.

Doubling can give you some interesting new possibilities, though note that doing this with woodwinds doesn't mean the resulting sound will double in volume.

Feel free to experiment, but below are three favored woodwind combinations:

• Flute and Oboe

• Oboe and Clarinet

• Flute and Clarinet

Chord Voicings

A chord voicing describes how you arrange the pitches in a chord. On a piano, if you played C-E-G, those notes are close together: that's a "closed" voicing. Play the notes of that chord as C-G-E and they are much more spread out: that's an "open" voicing.

Example 8a:

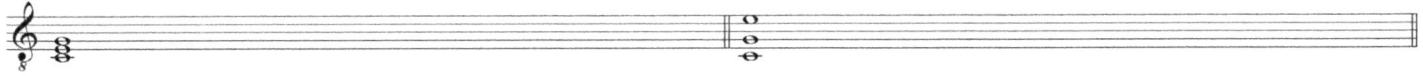

One of the biggest mistakes made when writing and orchestrating with samples in a home studio is for the composer to play orchestral voicings the same way they would play a piano chord.

This could become a lengthy section, so allow me to instead make a couple of simple generalizations. If you're relatively new to orchestration, this will help avoid some of the most common mistakes:

1. In general, you want to keep voicings open in the low end (i.e. keep the notes of a chord wider apart), and use tighter, "closed" voicings in the upper registers.

2. Doubling too many thirds in a chord is a common mistake. Yes, this works great in a lot of piano and guitar music, but you don't have to hammer home the third in orchestral section playing.

If you want to explore the reasons for these points in more depth, look into the overtone series (also called the harmonic series). It's often seen as a blueprint for effective chord voicings. I've decided not to go into it here as I want this book to be about composing for TV, rather than music theory! However, if you do look at the overtone series you'll see the bigger intervals used at the lower end of things, followed by smaller and smaller intervals as we get higher. When creating orchestral chords you want to keep that same spacing in mind: putting large intervals and the bottom and smaller intervals at the top.

Below are two examples of well structured chords. Notice the larger intervals at the low end and higher ones at the top, as well as how the chords aren't overrun by thirds.

Example 8b:

"You can't necessarily take a piano part and turn it into a string arrangement. Good string arrangement is done in a certain way where you respect the intervals between the different strings and you end up having this sound that we find pleasing.

The same goes with other types of instruments that I would use in a cue. There's always a bit of experimentation. I may come up with a few different parts and they feel like they're sitting well: I've got something doing the low frequencies, I've got something that's holding the midrange, maybe a melody is up in the higher frequencies and that seems to be feeling pretty good. But it feels like it need something else in one section and so now I'm trying to find another part that's going to give it that. And If I add something that is adding a lot of low frequency to something that already has low frequency then it sounds too muddy and the new part isn't doing much.

So it's a little bit of experimentation to try to get things to fit." – Mac Quayle

Balancing The Orchestral Mix

One of the advantages of samples is that you can choose whether to prioritize the goal of realism, or to use the wealth of control that samples give you to make things sound pretty much however you want them to, if that suits your project better.

If the goal is to make your MIDI orchestra sound as realistic as possible, you'll find many people have their own favorite techniques. Many choose to zero the reverb settings on the samples and then bus everything to the same reverb. Some pan elements of the orchestra, so they appear to sound in the same geographical positions they would be if you were listening in an auditorium.

One factor to consider, if realism is your goal, is the balance of instruments within the orchestra. If you were writing a track where the full orchestra was playing loudly, and you decided to put a clarinet solo in there, in real life the clarinet would get drowned out by the louder instruments around it. Yet with samples, you can simply boost the volume of the clarinet over the top of everything else. Yes, you have the control to do that, but in doing so, you'll be creating an unrealistic sound.

Unlike mixing a band, the orchestral sound we are all used to is created from the acoustic balance between instruments that the orchestra and the conductor create, along with the inherent volume capabilities of each instrument and section.

In his book *The Principles Of Orchestration*, Rimsky-Korsakov shares a useful tool regarding the strength of the different orchestral elements:

> *"In the most resonant group, the brass, the strongest instruments are the trumpets, trombones and tuba. In loud passages the horns are only one-half as strong, 1 Trumpet = 1 Trombone = 1 Tuba = 2 Horns. Woodwind instruments, in forte (loud) passages, are twice as weak as the horns, 1 Horn = 2 Clarinets = 2 Oboes = 2 Flutes = 2 Bassoons; but, in piano passages, all wind-instruments, wood or brass are of fairly equal balance.*

> *It is more difficult to establish a comparison in resonance between woodwind and strings, as everything depends on the number of the latter, but, in an orchestra of medium formation, it may be taken for granted that in piano (quiet) passages, the whole of one department (all 1st Violins or all 2nd Violins etc.) is equivalent in strength to one wind instrument, (Violins I = 1 Flute etc.), and, in forte passages, to two wind instruments, (Violins I = 2 Flutes = 1 Oboe + 1 Clarinet, etc.)."* (quoted from Nicolay Rimsky-Korsakov, *Principles of Orchestration, Édition Russe de Musique*, Paris, 1922).

He gives us what essentially are the ratios between the strength of different instrument groups. You might draw from this the conclusion that there are "volume points" that could be allocated:

- One woodwind instrument = 1

- One group of strings (e.g. first violins) = 2

- One Horn = 2

- One Brass Instrument = 4

Rimsky-Korsakov goes on to point out there are, of course, plenty of exceptions to be factored in, such as sustaining instruments versus short notes, and perhaps most importantly, the dynamic range that each section is playing in (he points out that the above observations are related to the orchestra playing loudly).

So it's worth observing that these ratios aren't foolproof. Certainly, each section could be instructed to play at a volume that most other instruments could rise above. However, it is worth having these natural balance ratios in mind when mixing your orchestral samples to make your samples sound even more realistic in the context of one another.

Final Thoughts

Remember that when you write for orchestra, you don't need to use all the sections, all of the time! Experiment with the textures and colors of different sections and, more importantly than anything else, go and listen to and analyze your favorite orchestral soundtracks to see how composers and orchestrators are making their pieces work.

Once again, you wouldn't feel the need to use every patch on a synth in a track, so you don't need to use all the sounds the orchestra has to offer in your track!

If your goal is to get your samples to sound as realistic as possible, confine yourself to what an orchestra can do. If you've got lots of cellos playing an ostinato, it's best to avoid trying to write more cello lines on top of that. Yes, the beauty of samples is that you could break the rules in this way, but in general, it will lead to an unrealistic sound and disrupt the natural balance between instruments, as well as potentially overcrowding the timbres and frequency ranges of your piece in that area.

Finally, give instruments room.

This may be seen as a general production tip as much as an orchestration one, but whatever type of music you are creating, orchestral influenced or otherwise, let your instrumental choices (and their ranges) make room for one another, to allow a track to breathe. This is especially important for TV soundtracks where less is often more.

Chapter Nine – Long Form And Short Form Track Versions

"Sometimes I'll get asked to write a cue and it's short. It's a short little piece that lasts thirty seconds or something. And I wrote something that I think turned out great and it's different from anything else I've written so far for that project, so it seems a shame for it to only have this thirty second version. That's maybe not going to be so useful to the editors when they want to do something longer with it.

So then I go ahead and do a longer version that will be a minute and a half, or two minutes long and turn that in. Then they'll have it there if they want to cut it up and do some other things with it.

And sometimes I'll just do it if I like it. If I think, 'Oh, this seems to be working well, I think it will be useful for them if they have the longer version,' then I'll make the longer version. Because then ultimately it will make my life easier when they're able to cut the longer version into a scene and sometimes it may just work, just like that.

And then there's one cue I don't have to write." – Mac Quayle

At times, when creating the soundtrack to a TV show, it may be advantageous for you to create a long form or short form version of an existing track or new idea. In this chapter I'll guide you through how to do this. We'll think about scenarios where the need for these different versions may arise and when this may, or may not, be a savvy use of your time.

Short Form Track Versions

From time to time I find that creating short form versions of ideas can be a useful and efficient way to work on several stages of the scoring process.

To me, a short form version (perhaps under 30 seconds in length) serves as a mood sketch: a taster of what you're imagining, so that the production team can understand. It's so hard to put music into words that often a little flavor of an idea can get something across.

Sometimes I'm in the thick of scoring a show and I have a list of several sequences that I need to work on. During this time, I might find myself unsure of quite what direction to take a certain scene in. Perhaps the director has said that they're not that happy with the temp music. If that's the case, I might score a small section of the scene and send it over to the production team for their feedback, while I continue work on other scenes.

A short taster of an idea might also be useful if I feel there is an alternate direction we could take the music in, which might be a curveball compared to what the team has asked me for. Scoring just a short section of the footage like this means we can consider alternative angles without taking up too much of anyone's time. This has the added benefit of reassuring the production team that you've put the majority of your time into what was asked of you, and less into your own experimentation.

So short form versions are all about being pressed for time and wanting to test other options. They are especially useful when the project in question will require a sizeable amount of your time to write, produce and orchestrate.

If you are submitting short form versions as ideas to the production team ahead of scoring the show, as aural "mood boards" of what might work, you can always then create longer form versions of the ideas that resonate. Discuss this with your director ahead of time and check that they like to work in this way. Some don't!

Long Form Track Versions

If the thinking behind short form track versions is to communicate ideas while saving everyone time, the idea behind creating long form track versions is to assist editors by giving them the ability to chop up and experiment with your track in their cuts.

Once it's "all hands on deck" at the latter stages of scoring you may well find that you're busy solely getting the required cues done and out there. Michael Price notes that, for the projects he works on, it's unlikely he'll be asked for any varying length versions once things have got going. The need for an edit of a different length at this point will usually be in reaction to a specific issue with the cut:

> *"There can be certain occasions, particularly up against a tight schedule, where maybe on the dub a cue or two will get swapped around, but that tends to be bounced back to you. So either I'm at the dub (and somebody tells me to my face that that cue is not working!) or I'm not and somebody has the good grace to phone me up just before I get fired! [joke!]*

> *So for drama, you're pretty much working to a tight cue sheet and the production are expecting you to hit every cue and they're not expecting to move much around themselves."*

Similarly, Walter Murphy may submit alternate length versions occasionally, but again for quite specific situations:

> *"He [a member of the show's production team], had asked me to stop the music at a certain point in the scene, but I thought it should have gone to the end of the scene. So I gave him the options."*

I find sending long form versions mostly has its place at the start of the production schedule.

There is some debate amongst TV composers about how much writing to do before you see any footage. Many people argue that writing before this period is wasted time, as much (sometimes all) of what you write may never be used. There is also a case to say that if you use up your energies too soon you may not be writing at your best when it matters, which is towards the end of the schedule.

While these are valid points, I personally feel that they are usually the viewpoint of the experienced composer, or a composer who knows clearly what kind of music he'll need to be writing – perhaps someone scoring the second or third season of a drama, or writing for a long running show.

Certainly, when watching Walter Murphy work in the studio, I was aware that, having written music for several seasons of *Family Guy* and *American Dad*, he knew the exactly the sound and musical requirements for that show as well as anyone on the production team did.

However, for those in the early part of their careers or coming onto a new show, I think getting some ideas together ahead of time can be important to establish what kind of music the production team like and would deem to be usable. Once you have sent a few ideas as shorter form versions (30 to 60 seconds), that the team like, you may decide to make longer versions of them.

A Guide To Creating Long Form Versions

When creating long form versions of your tracks for editors to chop up and experiment with, there are a few approaches that may prove particularly valuable:

Don't come in all at once

The reason for this is to provide options. If the editor wants an all-in start, they can grab that from later on in the track. So give them one element at a time. Remember, the goal here isn't to make a track that works primarily as a standalone piece, it's a chop-able ream of options which they can put together as they see fit.

No fade beginnings, no fade endings

Editors can fade things themselves. They need you to give them what they can't create on their own.

Four- to eight-bar sections usually work best

Give editors a good chunk of a section to use before it changes, but there's no need to let things go on longer than necessary!

Use some of the ideas in Chapter Six

For example, add subtle layers of interest when repeating sections.

Include a breakdown

Include a breakdown section and then build things up again.

Create sections that connect well

By creating different sections that can easily weave their endings/starts in and out of each other, you are giving the editor maximum flexibility. For example, it's a shame when editors find they can go from section A into section B and section C, but not from section C back into section A.

As with all aspects of this creative process, good preparation and flexibility will stand you in good stead for success.

Further Study

I sincerely hope that you have enjoyed reading this book, feel equipped with some valuable tools, and have absorbed a wealth of tools, techniques and ideas that you can take and apply to your own music.

If you're inspired to explore composition for TV further, with the aim of starting to make a part-time or full-time income from this medium, I've also created an online course you might be interested in, which is centered around an area of the business known as Library Music.

Library music (also called production music), is soundtrack music created by composers, but not to picture. These tracks are licensed from composers by music libraries, who then sell on and license this "off-the-shelf" music to production companies.

It's often the case that most of today's successful TV composers have a multitude of tracks licensed with music libraries, which generate royalty revenues for them in-between TV scoring projects. Writing for music libraries can also build your credits as a composer, especially if your library tracks are chosen for use on multiple shows.

As a result, writing library music can be a great path towards a career as a TV composer, as well providing a substantial part-time or full-time income.

The "Library Music That Sells" online course will teach you how to write, produce and mix great production music, educate you on the business side of the industry, explain how to form the connections you need with major music libraries and covers many more topics. Contributors include major label music library executives, award winning picture editors (telling you what elements they look for in TV music) and six-figure-a-year composers sharing their formulas and career paths.

As a reader of this book, I'd like to offer you the chance to sign up for three free video lessons at

www.musicforincome.com/introbook

This link will also give you a discount on the course, should you decide it's right for you. Otherwise, please just enjoy the free lessons!

Michael Kruk

Michael Price

Michael Price is one of the UK's most sought after composers. His critically acclaimed debut album on Erased Tapes Records, *Entanglement*, released in April 2015, was described as "gorgeous" by Rolling Stone, as "a neo-classical treat" by Uncut, and Clash remarked that "the emotional clout of this music is quite staggering". A new album, *Tender Symmetry*, was released on August 31st 2018. This ambitious musical project takes in a series of iconic National Trust locations across England as its inspiration, turning them into unlikely recording spaces.

Michael's work for film and television has been widely recognized, winning an Emmy® award in 2014, and Royal Television Society, Music&Sound, and Televisual Bulldog awards as well as a BAFTA nomination and two further Emmy® nominations for the critically acclaimed BBC series *Sherlock*, which he scores with David Arnold. Other upcoming TV projects include the fourth season of BAFTA-winning crime drama *Unforgotten* and the BBC's new Dracula adaptation, created by Stephen Moffat and Mark Gatiss.

Prior to achieving acclaim as a composer himself, Michael enjoyed significant achievements as a music editor on a number of blockbuster films such as Peter Jackson's *The Lord of the Rings* trilogy, Richard Curtis' *Love Actually, Bridget Jones: The Edge of Reason* and Alfonso Cuaron's *Children of Men*. As a music editor, Michael has been nominated for four MPSE Golden Reel Awards, winning in 2001 for *The Lord of the Rings: The Fellowship of the Ring*.

Michael's first film experience was as musical assistant, co-producer and arranger to the late Michael Kamen, with whom he collaborated for five years. During this time Michael worked on a number of prestigious projects including *X-Men, Band of Brothers, The Iron Giant, Metallica – S&M*, and live concerts around the world. Michael has also arranged or written additional music on a number of major film projects, including Edgar Wright's *Hot Fuzz, Tinker, Tailor, Soldier, Spy, Casino Royale* and *Quantum of Solace*.

Having studied there as an undergraduate, Michael has recently been appointed Visiting Professor of Composition on the Tonmeister Course at the University of Surrey, and is a full member of BAFTA, BASCA, MU, PRS and ASCAP.

Website: **www.michaelpricemusic.com**

Walter Murphy

Award winning composer Walter Murphy has been nominated for five Emmy® Awards, winning for the song, *You've Got A Lot To See*, from *Family Guy*. He was nominated for an Oscar for *Everybody Needs A Best Friend* from the movie *Ted* and nominated for three Grammy Awards, winning for *A Fifth Of Beethoven* from *Saturday Night Fever*. Walter was also nominated for two animation Annie Awards and has received many ASCAP and BMI Top Screen Music awards spanning his career.

Working with a 60-piece orchestra each week, Walter continues to showcase his ability to write music in all styles and in all genres for the FOX hit shows *Family Guy* and *American Dad*. He composed the theme songs to both shows and continues to compose the series' underscores.

Along with television, Walter has also collaborated with Seth MacFarlane on two of his movie projects, *Ted* and *Ted 2*. Working with an 80-piece orchestra for both features, he composed romantic comedy-adventure scores which included the Oscar nominated song, *Everybody Needs A Best Friend*, sung by Norah Jones.

Other projects include Warner Brothers' *Looney Tunes Feature Cartoons*, the theme and underscore to FOX series *The Cleveland Show*, and the NBC special *How Murray Saved Christmas*, garnering another Emmy® nomination for the song *You Gotta Believe*.

Walter has composed the underscore for the FOX/WB series, *Buffy, The Vampire Slayer* as well as for the long running ABC series *The Commish*. For Interscope Records, he composed, arranged and co-produced the Grammy nominated album, *Family Guy Live In Vegas*. He has also conducted his music and songs for live *Family Guy* performances in Los Angeles, Caesar's Palace in Las Vegas and Carnegie Hall in New York.

Born and raised in New York, Walter studied the organ and classical and jazz piano, composing for his high school band and orchestra. Accepted to the Manhattan School of Music as a composition major, he studied with Nicolas Flagello and Ludmila Ulehla, graduating with a degree in composition. While in college he composed and arranged for Doc Severinsen and *The Tonight Show* orchestra. He also released his first record, *A Fifth of Beethoven* which became a hit and was later featured in the film, *Saturday Night Fever*. It received a Grammy nomination and a win for him.

Website: **www.waltermurphy.com**

Mac Quayle

Audiences worldwide have been captivated by the unique musical stylings of Emmy® winning and Grammy nominated composer, Mac Quayle. He currently scores USA network's Golden Globe winning suspense-thriller *Mr Robot*, starring Christian Slater and Rami Malek, for which Mac won an Emmy®. Most recently, Mac received two Emmy® nominations for his main title and score for his music in Ryan Murphy's hit series, *FX's Feud: Bette and Joan*. Additionally, he received his second consecutive world soundtrack award nomination for his work on *Feud: Bette and Joan*, *Mr Robot* and *Scream Queens*.

He is currently composing the music for *American Horror Story: Cult*, and *The Assassination of Gianni Versace: American Crime Story*. He has been scoring *American Horror Story* since season 4 and scored FX's Emmy-winning *The People vs O.J. Simpson* starring John Travolta, Sarah Paulson and Cuba Gooding Jr.

Quayle has written music for over 40 films and television shows, and has accumulated a long list of credits as a music producer, dance re-mixer and multi-instrumentalist. His music can also be heard on a diverse list of feature films and documentaries.

Mac's music as an additional composer for Cliff Martinez can also be heard in HBO's Emmy-winning *The Normal Heart*, Film District's Critic's Choice Award-winning *Drive*, Warner Bros.' *Contagion* and A24's *Spring Breakers*.

As a producer, re-mixer and keyboardist, Mac has worked on over 300 releases, 40 #1 Billboard Dance hits, and earned a Grammy nomination for producing Donna Summer's *I Will Go with You*. Quayle has been awarded numerous Gold and Platinum records, as well as worked with some of the biggest names in the music business. Mac has created music for Madonna, Whitney Houston, Depeche Mode, Britney Spears, Elvis Presley, Annie Lennox, New Order, Beyonce and Sting, to name a few.

When asked about his career highlights, Mac responded, "I have been fortunate to work with so many talented people over the years. However, there is one special moment that stands out for me: playing ping pong with Peter Gabriel at Real World Studios."

Mac lives, works and plays ping pong in the mountains near Los Angeles.

Website: **www.macquayle.com**

How I Got My First Composing Job

I hope you've found this insight into writing effective music for TV helpful and informative – but the question remains: how does one go about getting those jobs in the first place?

Before I tell you how I got into the industry, I need you to understand something really important: someone else's route into this industry probably won't be yours. The fact is, there are many different scenarios that could lead to you scoring a TV show. People tend to obsess about finding a certain "way in" which they've heard about, or that their favourite composer took – but there is no magic bullet. My advice is to try a few approaches, keep an open mind, be persistent, and your chance will come along. And when it comes, be ready. This is a very relational industry, so be pro-active and get your music and yourself out there, in front of people.

A few years back, when I had no credits to my name, I set about trying to find directors in London. I did some research online and collected what contact details I could find, then reached out to people to ask if I could be of use to them. Over 80% never came back to me. This is normal and to be expected, though it was hard not to take it personally at the time. Those who did told me they'd keep my details "on file". If you don't get a closed door, then you can find a pleasant way of touching base with them every few months. Often, it's about timing. If they are currently looking for someone, and you happen to send them some tracks that are the type of thing they're looking for, you could get a shot at pitching for the show.

I'd had some correspondence with a guy who was working as an assistant director on several shows for a production company. He asked me for some recommendations for music for one of the shows and, while it was clear they weren't looking to hire a composer, I went out of my way to help him as much as I could. Soon after, he landed his first directing gig and asked me if I wanted to pitch for the show against some other composers. The production company sent me a couple of scenes from the show to write music to and eventually decided to take a chance on me.

You may well ask, don't they always want someone with experience? This would seem to make sense. However, if the production company points out your lack of experience (and you should never lie about this kind of thing), you can politely but confidently fight your corner. You may not have the credentials of some other composers, but that makes you a fresh sound and a different approach for their show. Plus, when someone is giving you a break, then your work ethic will be unsurpassed. (Please make sure your work ethic is unsurpassed!) I believe that if your music sounds great, then people will at least be interested in talking to you further about the job.

Lastly, I'd advise all up and coming TV composers to spend time writing for production music libraries while they are searching for that first TV show to score. Writing "off the shelf" music that can be used by TV shows that don't have a composer can hone your skills. It also demonstrates to a potential employer that your music has been used on TV before.

If you're interested in exploring production music further, go to:

www.musicforincome.com/introbook

Appendix – Equipment: The Basics

Gone are the days of huge studio setups with large mixing desks. I've scored several TV shows "in the box" (using only the sounds from the samples on my computer) that have aired to millions of viewers around the world. I've also worked on scores with a handful of musicians through to full orchestras. Musicians and big studios are great if the budget is there, but often the budget is being spent elsewhere, so the music you make from your home studio better sound pretty great. The good news is that nowadays there are plenty of options to allow you to do just that. Let's look at the essentials that you'll need.

Your Computer and DAW (Digital Audio Workstation)

Your DAW is the main software programme you'll use to make music. At the time of writing, Logic and Cubase lead the way, with notable nods to Pro Tools (previously known more for it's live audio recording capabilities), Studio One, Digital Performer and Ableton Live. I've heard composers get stunning results from all of these DAWs. The best DAW for you is often the one you feel most comfortable with. If you are just starting on the journey, Logic or Cubase may be best the options, due to their enormous global user base.

Your computer and DAW choices may be linked (Logic is Apple only, Cubase is more widely used by PC owners). When selecting a computer for your home studio, get the fastest processor and most RAM you can afford.

Audio Interface

An audio interface will allow you to record audio sources either directly (e.g. plugging in an electric guitar) or via a connected microphone. The interface gets the audio into your computer, then its outputs route the resulting music to your studio monitor speakers. The quality of your audio interface can make a significant difference to the quality of your recordings and playback. You most likely won't need an interface capable of simultaneously recording several instruments at once (you can overdub in your DAW), so I recommend a good quality one that can record one or two instruments at the same time. Your budget will usually dictate your choices, but for home studios I like audio interfaces from Universal Audio and Apogee. Also worth checking out are Mackie, Focusrite and Arturia. There are plenty of other good, budget friendly options as well as these makes.

Monitor Speakers and Headphones

The monitor speakers and headphones you need for your home studio are not the same as hifi speakers or recreational headphones. Hifi speakers and recreational headphones often "color" the sound, enhancing certain frequencies (usually the highs and lows). That's the last thing you want as composer/producer in your home studio. You want to know that the music you are hearing is honest and un-colored. Otherwise, when you send a producer your final mix, it might not sound the same to them as it does to you.

Go for the best monitor speakers you can afford, but always A/B test a few monitors before buying. Take a piece of music to play that you know very well and play it on all the monitors you are deciding between. Resist the temptation to listen to monitors outside of your budget! Let your ears rest for a few minutes, then go back and listen again.

For home studios I like monitors from Focal, Adam Audio and Genelec. Notable mentions also go to Neumann, Yamaha, Mackie, KRK and M-Audio. Again, there are plenty of options besides these makes, especially when you get into the higher price ranges.

Headphones are great for writing music on the go if you have a laptop, are working late or want another point of reference for your mix. Personally, I always have a set of studio headphones in my home studio, but never write just using them. Check out professional studio headphone lines from companies such as Sennheiser, Audio-Technica, Beyerdynamic, Sony and AKG.

Samples

Your samples are your computer generated sounds. If you're not recording live audio, these samples will be the instruments that make up your compositions. DAWs often ship with a basic set of samples, but the more your music needs samples of real instruments (strings, brass, guitars, etc.) as opposed to electronic sources (synths, etc.) the more you're going to need good samples.

A lot of TV music today is "orchestral hybrid" – a mixture of real orchestral instruments and electronically generated sounds. Companies such as Spitfire, Project SAM and 8DIO offer exceptional orchestral sample packs that are well worth investing in. Keep your eye out for sales on these products each year.

The other side of orchestral hybrid music is the electronic aspect. Software such as Spectrasonics Omnisphere and offerings by other companies such as Native Instruments offer relatively easy to use interfaces that can inspire your writing and create great sounding TV soundtracks.

Music soundtracks often follow trends, so make sure that your samples (and how you use them) don't become dated. This is less of a problem with orchestral samples (as long as yours sound great to begin with), but keep your ear to the ground regarding new sample packs from sample companies, so that your music keeps up with current trends.